Introduction to the Book of Ezekiel

Introduction to the Book of Ezekiel

Reading Ezekiel in Ruins and Renewal

under the supervision of
Soo Kim Sweeney

Theological Essentials

©Digital Theological Library 2025
Library of Congress Cataloging-in-Publication Data

Soo Kim Sweeney (creator).
Introduction to the Book of Ezekiel: Reading Ezekiel in Ruins and Renewal
/ Soo Kim Sweeney
156 + x pp. cm. 12.7 x 20.32
ISBN 979-8-89731-997-8 (Print)
ISBN 979-8-89731-174-3 (Ebook)
ISBN 979-8-89731-169-9 (Kindle)
ISBN 979-8-89731-186-6 (Abridged Audio Discussion)
    1.   Bible. Ezekiel—Criticism, interpretation, etc.
    2.   Bible. Ezekiel—Theology
    3.   Bible. Ezekiel—Study and teaching
BS1545.52 .S94 2025

This book is available in other languages at www.DTLPress.com

Cover Image: The "chariot vision" of Ezekiel by Matthäus Merian (1593–1650)

Contents

Part III
Living with Ezekiel

Series Preface

Artificial Intelligence (AI) is changing everything, including theological scholarship and education. This series, *Theological Essentials*, is designed to bring the creative potential of AI to the field of theological education. In the traditional model, a scholar with both mastery of the scholarly discourse and a record of successful classroom teaching would spend several months — or even several years — writing, revising and rewriting an introductory text which would then be transferred to a publisher who also invested months or years in production processes. Even though the end product was typically quite predictable, this slow and expensive process caused the prices of textbooks to balloon. As a result, students in developed nations paid more than they should have for the books and students in developing nations typically had no access to these (cost-prohibitive) textbooks until they appeared as discards and donations decades later. In previous generations, the need for quality assurance — in the form of content generation, expert review, copy-editing and printing time — may have made this slow, expensive and exclusionary approach inevitable. However, AI is changing everything.

This series is very different; it is created by AI. The cover of each volume identifies the work as "created under the supervision of" an expert in the field. However, that person is not an author in the traditional sense. The creator of each volume has been trained by the DTL staff in the use of AI and *the creator has used AI to create, edit, revise and recreate the text that you see*. With that creation process clearly identified, let me explain the goals of this series.

Our Goals:

Credibility: Although AI has made—and continues to make—huge strides over the last few years, no unsupervised AI can create a truly reliable or fully credible college or seminary level text. The limitations of AI generated content sometimes originates from the limitations of the content itself (the training set may be inadequate), but more often, user dissatisfaction with AI-generated content arises from human errors associated with poor prompt engineering. The DTL Press has sought to overcome both of these problems by hiring established scholars with widely recognized expertise to create books within their areas of expertise and by training those scholars and experts in AI prompt engineering. To be clear, the scholar whose name appears on the cover of this work has created this volume—generating, reading, regenerating, rereading and revising the work. Even though the work was generated (in varying degrees) by AI, the names of our scholarly creators appear on the cover as a guarantee that the content is equally credible with any introductory work which that scholar/creator would pen using the traditional model.

Stability: AI is generative, meaning that the response to each prompt is uniquely generated for that specific request. No two AI-generated responses are precisely the same. The inevitable variability of AI responses presents a significant pedagogical challenge for professors and students who wish to begin their discussions and analysis on the basis of a shared set of ideas. Educational institutions need stable texts in order to prevent pedagogical chaos. These books provide that stable text from which to teach, discuss and engage ideas.

Affordability: The DTL Press is committed to the idea that affordability should not be a barrier to knowledge. *All persons are equally deserving of the right to know and to understand.* Therefore, ebook versions of all DTL Press books are available from the DTL libraries without charge, and available as print books for a nominal fee. Our scholar/creators are to be thanked for their willingness to forego traditional royalty arrangements. (Our creators are compensated for their generative work, but they do not receive royalties in the traditional sense.)

Accessibility: The DTL Press would like to make high quality, low cost introductory textbooks available to everyone, everywhere in the world. The books in this series are immediately made available in multiple languages. The DTL Press will create translations in other languages upon request. Translations are, of course, generated by AI.

Our Acknowledged Limitations:

Some readers are undoubtedly thinking, "but AI can only produce derivative scholarship; AI can't create original, innovative scholarship." That criticism is, of course, largely accurate. AI is largely limited to aggregating, organizing and repackaging pre-existing ideas (although sometimes in ways that can be used to accelerate and refine the production of original scholarship). Still while acknowledging this inherent limitation of AI, the DTL Press would offer two comments: (1) Introductory texts are seldom meant to be truly ground breaking in their originality and (2) the DTL Press has other series dedicated to publishing original scholarship with traditional authorship.

Our Invitation:

The DTL Press would like to fundamentally reshape academic publishing in the theological world to make scholarship more accessible and more affordable in two ways. First, we would like to generate introductory texts in all areas of theological discourse, so that no one is ever forced to "buy a textbook" in any language. It is our vision for professors anywhere to be able to use one book, two books or an entire set of books in this series as the *introductory* textbooks for their classes. Second, we would also like to publish traditionally authored scholarly monographs for Open Access (free) distribution for an advanced scholarly readership.

Finally, the DTL Press is non-confessional and will publish works in any area of religious studies. Traditionally authored books are peer-reviewed; AI-generated introductory book creation is open to anyone with the required expertise to supervise content generation in that area of discourse. If you share the DTL Press's commitment to credibility, affordability and accessibility, contact us about changing the world of theological publishing by contributing to this series or a more traditionally authored series.

With high expectations,

Thomas E. Phillips

DTL Press Executive Director
www.thedtl.org
www.DTLpress.com

Introduction
Ezekiel as Scripture, Witness, and Challenge An Invitation to the Reader

This book is not intended to tame Ezekiel. Instead, it invites those willing to linger at the prophet's edge — where divine presence vibrates, where words are paused, and where theology unfolds through gesture and vulnerability. This volume does not offer a conventional commentary or a systematic doctrinal account. Instead, it provides an invitation to engage with Ezekiel through literary attentiveness, theological depth, ethical awareness, and pastoral encouragement.

We read Ezekiel not only because it is challenging, but also because its difficulty serves as a form of witness. The book does not yield easily to interpretation — it resists simplification, eludes neat categories, and demands sustained attention. In its silences, excesses, and ruptures, Ezekiel disorients to reveal. Yet, it also provides instruction. The book insists on God's presence amid collapse, on the prophet's burden as a sign, and on the remnant's vocation to imagine what comes next.

To read Ezekiel is, therefore, to risk transformation. Its metaphors disturb, its silences accuse, and its visions unsettle what we thought we knew about God and ourselves. Yet precisely in that dislocation lies its theological charge. The Book of Ezekiel is not simply a scroll of deferred speech; it is a prophetically engineered design, crafted to remember rupture, resist regression, and rehearse ethical restoration.

This volume traverses three interconnected arcs. Part I establishes rhetorical strategies and theological displacements of the scroll. Part II delves into selected passages to explore Ezekiel's internal logic and external challenges—its composition, metaphors, and prophetic performance. Part III considers the ethical and homiletic futures that emerge from the Book of Ezekiel—not only through its content but through its construction, guiding reflection on trauma, memory, and preaching. In this manner, the Book of Ezekiel is approached as a dynamic landscape—textual, spatial, and theological—where speech and silence intersect to delineate the possibilities of divine-human interaction.

To study Ezekiel, then, is not merely to observe a prophet from a distance. It is to be drawn into his orbit, and perhaps to be summoned as a witness in our own time.

Part I
Framing the Prophet and the Scroll

The book of Ezekiel opens not with a clear prophetic utterance, but with a disruptive vision. Rather than delivering a speech, the prophet is immersed in what he sees. Ezekiel 1 does not offer a gentle entry into prophetic vocation; it confronts us with an overwhelming experience of divine presence. This rupture serves not as a barrier to interpretation, but as its generative force. Meaning in Ezekiel arises not from narrative clarity, but from affective and symbolic intensity

Part I of this volume treats disorientation as a formative experience rather than an obstructive one. The silence, symbolism, and abundance found in Ezekiel's opening chapters require a distinct approach to reading — one that embraces uncertainty rather than seeking an immediate resolution. Theological tension should not be viewed as something to be overcome, but rather as a space to be experienced. Here, presence may not be reassuring, and communication may not always resonate. This section, then, invites the reader into a theology of interruption.

Chapter 1 lays the conceptual groundwork by exploring the scroll as a performative object. Prophecy in Ezekiel is not simply proclaimed — it is consumed, enacted, delayed, and embodied. Divine speech is abundant yet often goes unreceived. Symbolic action is vivid yet opaque. Ezekiel's prophetic identity is forged in this paradox of clarity and collapse.

Chapter 2 expands the scope by tracing how Ezekiel has been read, resisted, and reimagined across traditions. Rather than offering a singular interpretive framework, it presents a multivocal landscape — from Jewish mysticism and Christian allegory to Islamic references and contemporary scholarly reappraisals. These encounters form a kind of reception history that refuses reduction and demands theological humility.

Chapter 3 introduces a pragmatic-theological lens. It considers how the Book of Ezekiel functions not only as an ancient artifact but as a communicative text that continues to shape preaching, teaching, and lived reflection. By foregrounding the breakdown of communicative alignment between sender, messenger, message, and receiver, this chapter suggests that Ezekiel models not effective proclamation but the theological necessity of deferred transmission. The prophet becomes not simply a speaker but a site of divine interruption.

These three chapters in Part I collectively create a foundation that is informed by history, broad in interpretation, and grounded in theology. Ezekiel is not presented as a prophet of clear messages, but rather as a figure of disruption. His role calls for more than just understanding; it requires presence, patience, and ethical engagement.

Chapter 1
What Ezekiel Lacks, What Ezekiel Overflows With — and Why That Matters

Ezekiel does not draw the reader in with lyrical beauty or prophetic closeness. The book begins instead with rupture — an overwhelming vision without immediate explanation, a divine presence that embodies the overwhelming rationale for judgment. The prophet's early experiences — encounters with hybrid beings, the firmament, and the divine chariot — are presented with density rather than comfort. From the outset, the reader is confronted not with dialogue, but with distance; not with consolation, but with complexity. This chapter examines how Ezekiel's distinctive prophetic grammar — marked by absence, excess, and silence — constitutes a theology of estrangement. What is missing in the Book of Ezekiel is as significant as what overwhelms the text. This dynamic reframes divine-human communication not as clarity, but as confrontation.

What Ezekiel Lacks

The Book of Ezekiel notably lacks many of the literary and theological features found in other prophetic writings. There is a scarcity of lamentation, intercession, and almost no communal dialogue. Unlike Moses or Jeremiah, the prophet rarely advocates for the people. Ezekiel's silences are not merely narrative omissions; they constitute theological disruptions. His speech is delayed (3:26), public mourning is prohibited (24:17), and prayer is withheld. Even when divine speech is abundant, it often seems

5

performatively displaced: directed at unreachable audiences, conveyed in exile, and frequently without clear reception.

What is even more striking is the absence of certain elements: there are no clear petitions for forgiveness, no collective confessions, no joyful reunion, and no miraculous interventions. The prophet's dramatic life becomes the sole sign of the divine intervention. The public mourning for his deceased wife was prohibited (24:15–24), his actions go unrecorded, and his audience remains largely unresponsive. In exile, Ezekiel's people exist in a state of suspended time — dates may be recorded, but time is no longer lived. The cyclical rhythms of sacred festivals and seasonal rites have ceased, leaving no embodied experience of temporal flow or renewal. The prophet's precise time-stamping, then, reads less like a liturgical calendar and more like a survival ritual — as if, like Robinson Crusoe marking days on an island after shipwreck, Ezekiel is resisting the erasure of time by inscribing it into the sandbanks of historical collapse.

The performative excess in Ezekiel remains unfulfilled, thereby dramatizing the disjunction between divine intent and human consciousness. While the scroll is consumed, its contents remain unspecified. Repetitive refrains such as "they will know that I am YHWH" and temporal markers like "on that day" (*bayyôm hahû*) surface not as promises but rather as unresolved assertions. The reader encounters a revelation that, while overwhelming, ultimately withholds clarity. Despite numerous divine commands instructing Ezekiel to convey messages of judgment and perform symbolic acts, the Book of Ezekiel explicitly records actual communication to the people in only three instances — chapters 8–11, 12, and 24 — highlighting a striking scarcity of direct prophetic delivery. These communications emerge not as calls for repentance but as grim forecasts of imminent or unfolding doom. For the audience, such messages are perceived as retrospective warnings — arriving too late to make an effective change. This overabundance of symbolic scripting thus does not guide the community toward repentance but leaves it in a state of theological suspense.

This absence is not simply a void; rather, it serves as a frame that redirects the reader's focus from rhetorical persuasion to embodied interruption. By withholding expected prophetic gestures, the text destabilizes theological assumptions — particularly those associated with presence, access, and divine responsiveness. Ezekiel does not inhabit a communicative ecosystem; he traverses its remnants.

What Ezekiel Overflows With

In the absence of overt dialogue or confession, the Book of Ezekiel is characterized by a profound symbolic density. The text is replete with visions, metaphors, and performative commands, yet these elements often fail to meet the expectations established by traditional narrative structures. For instance, in chapter 4, Ezekiel receives instructions to lie on his side and consume defiled food. Still, the narrative notably refrains from confirming whether these actions are executed or merely conveyed. There exists a command without accompanying commentary and performance devoid of witness.

Crucially, YHWH in the book of Ezekiel is characterized by unyielding resolve. Although Ezekiel frequently receives divine commands to call the people to repentance, it is striking that the only three explicitly recorded instances of prophetic communication — chapters 8–11, 12, and 24 — contain no such call.

Instead, each of these moments delivers an unambiguous pronouncement of judgment. This raises a crucial question: is the book truly focused on urging repentance, or does it instead underscore the inevitability of judgment in the face of persistent resistance? In contrast to Isaiah's appeals to "return," Ezekiel presents a God who has already distanced Himself, choosing to manifest His actions not within the temple but among the exiles. Consequently, the text's symbolic richness does not serve to elucidate but rather to disturb. The pervasive themes of YHWH's anger and resolve toward His own people permeate nearly all judgment oracles, elucidating the reasons and mechanisms that led to the people's exile.

Furthermore, the text exhibits a notable prevalence of shame language, particularly manifest in gendered portrayals of Jerusalem in chapters 16 and 23. The city is rendered stripped, exposed, and humiliated — depicted grotesquely as a theological metaphor. The pairing of *kālam* (shame) with *kābôd* (glory), as articulated by Klopfenstein, indicates that shame transcends mere punishment; rather, it constitutes the paradoxical foundation upon which divine glory is reasserted. The overwhelming images presented in Ezekiel are not gratuitous; they mediate a theological understanding wherein glory is prefigured by disfigurement, and presence is anticipated through abasement.

Such symbolic excess necessitates ethical caution. While other prophetic figures utilize metaphor as a means of persuasion, Ezekiel often wields it as a mechanism of rupture. Shame, for example, is not merely expunged but is instead curated within the narrative framework. This saturation of symbolism renders the text both theologically significant and ethically contentious.

Why That Matters

Reading Ezekiel transforms one into a theological reader. The absence of dialogue and the abundance of visions compel readers to adopt a stance of endurance rather than mastery. Ezekiel reveals that divine revelation may not always align with human readiness; words may be spoken without an audience, and understanding may emerge only after a period of desolation.

The Book of Ezekiel serves as a mirror for exile — not just in the political sense, but also in terms of communication. Its structure reflects a state of theological suspension: what God articulates is preserved yet not fully received. The book anticipates an audience that is not present, moral clarity that remains elusive, and a future restoration that is not yet assured.

For those engaged in theological formation — preachers, educators, and readers — the implications are significant. This book cautions preachers against adhering strictly to the conventional formula of judgment-repentance-forgiveness-restoration. What does it mean to bear a message that is premature? How do we uphold a vision not for the present, but for an uncertain future?

Ezekiel's silence should not be misconstrued as passivity; rather, it serves as a witness. The abundant visions are not a sign of indulgence but a deliberate strategy. Moreover, the ruptures that the prophet experienced may represent divine thresholds.

Chapter 2
Ezekiel's Reception and Interpretation

From mystical ascent to editorial excision, from eschatological blueprints to ethical trauma, Ezekiel's scroll speaks in every age — and speaks back.

The Book of Ezekiel does not quietly settle into the interpretive traditions that surround it. It is a volatile scroll — too symbolic for the systematic theologian, too strange for liturgical comfort, and too violent for uncritical devotion. And yet, it has endured. This chapter traces Ezekiel's reception across time and tradition, not merely to identify where he has been influential, but to understand how and why he continues to provoke. Reception, in Ezekiel's case, is rarely passive. His readers do not merely interpret him; they are, in turn, interpreted by him.

Scholarly Trajectories

The Book of Ezekiel has generated a multifaceted scholarly discourse, ranging from allegorical interpretation and debates between priest and prophet to trauma theory and diasporic theology. This section outlines the diverse approaches that have emerged across historical and disciplinary lines, focusing not on linear progression but on ruptures, reconfigurations, and hermeneutical intensities.

In early Christian exegesis, Ezekiel was foundational for mystical and ecclesial frameworks. Origen's *Homilies on Ezekiel* (3rd c.) famously allegorized the *merkavah* (chariot) vision as the soul's ascent toward divine communion. Jerome's 4th-century *Commentariorum in Ezechielem Prophetam*

11

retained this mystical trajectory while emphasizing ecclesial typology. At the same time, Jewish mystical traditions such as *Hekhalot Rabbati* (late 4th–6th c.) appropriated Ezekiel's chariot as a heavenly cartography for spiritual ascent.

Rabbinic interpretation approached Ezekiel with reverence and caution. Saadia Gaon, Rashi, Ibn Ezra, and others worked to harmonize Ezekiel's temple vision (chs. 40–48) with Torah. Yet passages like *Mishnah Ḥagigah* 2:1 reflect hesitation about public engagement with the *merkavah* vision, underscoring the text's volatile sanctity. Meanwhile, Pseudo-Ezekiel fragments from Qumran recontextualized the prophet's visions within apocalyptic and messianic frameworks, adapting Ezekiel to foster ideological resilience amid political rupture.

In modern scholarship, historical-critical methods reshaped Ezekiel's role. Walther Zimmerli's *Hermeneia* commentaries (1969, 1979) integrated philological analysis with theological reflection, presenting Ezekiel as a priestly figure re-narrating Israel's memory. Moshe Greenberg emphasized pedagogical coherence and rhetorical unity across his two-volume *Anchor Bible* commentary (1983, 1997), countering fragmentary readings.

By contrast, Gustav Hölscher's 1924 commentary proposed a dramatic editorial excision, arguing that most priestly materials of the book were non-Ezekielian. His work crystallized the priest-prophet dichotomy that would dominate the field for decades. More recently, Marvin Sweeney (2013) has argued for a reconciliation of these roles, proposing that priestly and prophetic strands in Ezekiel are mutually constitutive, not contradictory.

Performative and literary readings have further reframed the scroll. Margaret Odell and Andrew Mein, for instance, interpret Ezekiel's symbolic acts as rhetorical performances rather than historical accounts, thereby shaping theology through enacted speech. Stephen Cook views the Gog oracles and temple visions (chs. 38–48) as liturgical blueprints that reimagine sacred order. Paul Joyce's ethical interpretation of Ezekiel 18 highlights the significance of moral agency within the context of exile. Meanwhile, Dalit Rom- Shiloni examines Ezekiel's rhetorical construction of a displaced identity, delving into inter-Israelite conflict and notions of spatial belonging.

Comparative approaches have also flourished. Daniel Bodi draws parallels between Ezekiel and the *Babylonian Poem of Erra*, situating Ezekiel within Mesopotamian mythic frameworks of divine wrath and urban devastation. Safwat Marzouk examines how Babylonian imperial mythology influences Ezekiel's depiction of Egypt as Leviathan. Tova Ganzel examines the temple vision as spatial-theological reconstruction in response to communal dislocation.

Feminist critics have powerfully challenged the ethical cost of Ezekiel's metaphors. Julie Galambush (1992) examines the theological violence inherent in the Jerusalem-as-wife imagery. Athalya Brenner scrutinizes chapters 16 and 23 through a lens of gendered trauma, arguing that Ezekiel's rhetoric requires ethical resistance, not merely exegetical sympathy.

Interdisciplinary models continue to expand the field. Rose Stevenson and Natalie Mylonas examine Ezekiel's spatial poetics as a form of theological architecture. C. A. Strine, C. L. Crouch, and Madhavi Nevader bring migration theory into dialogue with Ezekiel's diasporic imagination. These readings reframe the scroll as a survival manual, liturgical archive, and reterritorialized theology.

Trauma studies have brought further insight. Ellen Davis (1989) describes Ezekiel's silence and symbolism as symptoms of divine estrangement. Ruth Poser (2012) reads the book as trauma literature — its structure fractured, its imagery excessive, its narrative looping. She argues that Ezekiel does not resolve trauma but preserves its rupture.

Finally, communicative-performance models highlight Ezekiel's internal semiotic tensions. Soo Kim Sweeney proposes that the scroll operates as a medium of interrupted communication, where divine command, prophetic enactment, and audience reception are structurally misaligned. In this reading, Ezekiel is not a speaker but a bearer of fracture — his scroll a theological artifact of divine absence and prophetic witness.

Ezekiel in Religious Traditions
Jewish Traditions

In early Judaism, Ezekiel's imagery was at once revered and restricted. The *Mishnah* (*Ḥagigah* 2:1) warned against public exposition of Ezekiel 1, lest divine mysteries mislead or overwhelm the uninitiated. Nevertheless, Ezekiel profoundly shaped mystical trajectories. In *Hekhalot Rabbati* (late 4th–6th c.), the prophet's chariot vision becomes a celestial map — a guide to heavenly ascent and angelic realms.

Rabbinic midrash draws deeply from Ezekiel to interpret Jerusalem's destruction and envision its restoration. Medieval commentators, such as Rashi, Saadia Gaon, and Ibn Ezra, labored to reconcile Ezekiel's temple vision (chs. 40–48) with Torah prescriptions — often transforming contradictions into interpretive ingenuity. In modern Jewish theology, Moshe Greenberg, Marvin Sweeney, and Dalit Rom-

Shiloni treat Ezekiel as both a theological archive and an ethical provocation, addressing the traumas of exile, the construction of communal identity, and the spatialization of sanctity.

Visual exegesis also emerged early. At the Dura- Europos Synagogue (3rd c.), Ezekiel appears prominently in wall paintings, especially in the depiction of the dry bones vision (Ezek 37). These images represent one of the earliest Jewish visual theologies — a liturgical memory rendered in color, gesture, and space.

Christian Traditions

The New Testament does not quote Ezekiel as frequently as Isaiah or the Psalms, yet it draws deeply on his visions — particularly in scenes of resurrection, pastoral identity, and eschatological architecture. The Gospel writers, Paul and John the Seer, each take fragments of Ezekiel's prophetic grammar and recontextualize them to interpret the crucified and risen Christ, the life of the church, and the vision of new creation.

Ezekiel's vision of the valley of dry bones (37:1–14) dramatizes Israel's return from exile as bodily resurrection. The spirit (*rûah*) that enters the bones signals not merely national revival, but divine re-animation. Matthew 27:52–53 offers a startling narrative echo: following Jesus' death, "many bodies of the saints who had fallen asleep were raised," and "came out of the tombs after his resurrection and entered the holy city." This scene, unique to Matthew, collapses eschatological time, treating resurrection not only as Christological victory but as Israel's restoration in embodied form. Ezekiel's imagery of scattered bones reassembled by breath becomes, in Matthew, the visual grammar of apocalyptic fulfillment.

In Ezekiel 34, YHWH condemns the corrupt shepherds of Israel and promises to shepherd the flock himself. "I myself will search for my sheep," declares the divine voice (34:11). This theological indictment becomes Christological revelation in John 10, where Jesus proclaims, "I am the good shepherd" (10:11). The Johannine Jesus does not merely echo Ezekiel's concern for scattered sheep; he claims divine prerogative, assuming the role that YHWH had reserved for Himself. The prophetic promise of divine pastoral care is fulfilled in the incarnation — and ultimately, in a shepherd who lays down his life.

Paul's declaration that believers were "dead through trespasses and sins" (Eph 2:1) but have now been "made alive together with Christ" (2:5) resonates unmistakably with Ezekiel's vision of spiritual reanimation. Ezekiel's promise of a new heart and new spirit (36:26–27) undergirds Paul's theology of transformative grace. Where Ezekiel imagines Israel's rebirth as divine initiative in exile, Paul applies this language to Gentile and Jewish believers alike, framing salvation as resurrection from moral and spiritual death.

John's apocalyptic vision of the New Jerusalem is saturated with Ezekielian imagery. The measurements, rivers, and gates of Ezekiel's final chapters reappear transfigured in Revelation 21–22. Yet there is a theological shift: whereas Ezekiel's temple is marked by boundaries and regulated access, Revelation's city has "no temple in it, for its temple is the Lord God the Almighty and the Lamb" (Rev 21:22). The architecture of restriction becomes a theology of indwelling presence. The eschaton is not the restoration of cultic structures, but their dissolution into unmediated communion.

16

Taken together, these New Testament engagements with Ezekiel reflect continuity and transformation. Ezekiel's metaphors — resurrection, shepherding, spirit-infused life, and sacred space — become theological idioms through which early Christians articulate the meaning of Christ's death, resurrection, and the promise of new creation. Far from being a marginal prophet, Ezekiel becomes a canonical architect of eschatological imagination.

Christian interpretation of Ezekiel has long emphasized allegory, ecclesiology, and eschatology. In his *Homiliae in Ezechielem* (late 6th c.), Gregory the Great interpreted Ezekiel's struggles as a mirror of pastoral vocation — linking muteness, burden, and obedience to the Christian shepherd's labor. Medieval figures such as Rupert of Deutz and Richard of St. Victor interpreted the temple visions as heavenly liturgies, with architectural schematics designed to model divine order.

Mystical exegesis flourished as well. Dionysius the Carthusian (15th c.) viewed Ezekiel as a contemplative guide, while monastic readers used the chariot vision to explore the tension between divine transcendence and mystical union.

The Reformation revived interest in prophetic critique. John Calvin emphasized Ezekiel's prophetic authority and theological sovereignty, reading the text through the lens of covenantal judgment. Lutheran and Reformed theologians such as Johannes Cocceius and William Greenhill spiritualized the temple vision, interpreting it as typological anticipation of ecclesial renewal.

Christian art absorbed and refracted these interpretations. William Blake's *Ezekiel's Vision* (early 19th c.) reimagines the chariot in radical Romantic form — depicting divine-human encounter as cosmic drama. Apocalyptic traditions, particularly dispensationalist theology, continue to align Ezekiel's temple with the New Jerusalem of *Revelation* 21–22, reading the prophet as eschatological architect.

Islamic Traditions

Although Ezekiel (Ḥizqīl) is not mentioned by name in the Qur'an, his presence echoes in classical Islamic literature. Tafsīr traditions associate him with verses like Q 2:243 and Q 36:78–79, in which God revives the dead to display divine power. Classical commentators such as al-Ṭabarī and al-Thaʿlabī identify Ezekiel as the prophet in the "Valley of the Dry Bones" episode, interpreting his mission as proof of resurrection and divine mercy.

In *Qiṣaṣ al-Anbiyāʾ* ("Stories of the Prophets"), Ezekiel appears as a wise and pious messenger, sometimes portrayed as a military and moral reformer in times of national peril. His association with restoration, bodily resurrection, and cosmic renewal places him in the center of Islamic theologies of eschatology and divine intervention.

Prophet, Priest, Pastor: Learning with Ezekiel

For modern readers—including students, preachers, and theological communities—Ezekiel presents a series of challenging questions: What does it mean to speak when no one is listening? What becomes of the priesthood for one called to serve as a priest when the temple lies in ruins? What is the essence of preaching when words are overshadowed by judgment?

Ezekiel is not reducible to a single role. He is a messenger without reply, a scribe of sacred trauma, and a watchman whose warning is archived rather than received. He is at once prophet, priest, and pastor—but in none of these roles does he offer stability or resolution. Instead, his ministry exemplifies endurance in the face of dissonance.

In the classroom, Ezekiel invites students to examine and challenge theological binaries. Why assume conflict between priestly ritual and prophetic spontaneity? Why interpret "pastoral" care as merely soft or soothing? Ezekiel's vocation subverts these assumptions. His silence is not passive; it is a disciplined witness. His visions are not wild ecstasies but structured performances of rupture. Students are challenged to reconsider not just what a prophet is, but what it means to remain faithful amid failure.

In the pulpit, Ezekiel speaks to those who carry messages no one wants to hear. His model of proclamation thus becomes not persuasive but preservative. The preacher does not convince, but he is the one who remembers, who testifies to what was seen and heard when God spoke and the people were not ready to listen. Ezekiel's ministry is not vindicated by outcome but by presence. He embodies the truth that not all speech is meant to succeed, and not all silence is absent.

Conclusion

Throughout the centuries, the figure of Ezekiel has faced resistance, undergone restructuring, and been reimagined in various ways. Gustav Hölscher sought to impose coherence on the scroll, while others have chosen to embrace its inherent tensions. Ezekiel has been depicted on synagogue walls, resonated within monastic liturgies, and infused Christian apocalyptic architecture. He is not a prophet of closure but a catalyst for provocation.

His scroll does not yield a singular theology; rather, it presents a cascade of interruptions: mystical, traumatic, eschatological, and ethical. He is a prophet who deconstructs in order to redefine; who silences to create space; who speaks not for the sake of resolution, but to prompt our attention.

Ultimately, Ezekiel's scroll is unfinished. It remains open—not to be completed, but to be carried forward.

Chapter 3
Reading Ezekiel from Pragmatic Perspectives

What does prophecy look like when the audience is missing, and the words are archived for an unknown future? Ezekiel's world is not dialogical but custodial — where communication does not seek instant effect but long-term integrity. This chapter builds on the interpretive foundations of Chapters 1 and 2, now asking: What do Ezekiel's 'prophetic speeches' mean to readers and interpreters? We engage the Book of Ezekiel not only as a text to be studied but as a performative agent — one that reorders categories of presence, responsibility, and transmission.

Rather than functioning as a real-time conversation between the prophet and the people, the Book of Ezekiel stages divine speech as deferred inscription. The prophet is told repeatedly that the people will not listen (2:5; 3:7). Yet the scroll must still be recorded. This creates a theology of archival prophecy, where the value of divine speech lies not in its immediate reception but in its preservation across ruptures. The role of the prophet evolves from merely serving as a messenger of divine revelation to embodying the function of a custodian of divine will.

This transformation underscores a profound shift in the nature of prophetic discourse, wherein the prophet engages in the intricate process of inscribing wisdom into the silence of history. This act of writing is not merely an echo of the present but a hopeful testament to a future where the carefully crafted scrolls are destined to be unveiled, interpreted, and appreciated for their transformative insights. The prophet, therefore, becomes a steadfast guardian of these sacred texts, anticipating a time when their words will resonate with understanding and purpose in a world yet to grasp their significance fully. Ezekiel's communicative structure is profoundly asymmetric:

Sender: YHWH, whose speech is frequent but strategically staged.

Messenger: Ezekiel, often mute, always scripted.

Receiver: A fragmented audience—Jerusalem's remnants, exiles in Babylon, or future generations.

We can view this imbalance as the book's distinctive theological strategy rather than a shortcoming. The book does not portray YHWH to correct the audience's deafness; instead, God transforms his speech into gesture, time into waiting, and prophecy into archive. The message is not "delivered" but ritualistically stored. The communicative breakdown is thus repurposed as a prophetic vocation.

Once we adopt this perspective, Ezekiel's silence (3:26) becomes a theological event rather than simply a constraint. It creates the possibility that faithful speech can be delayed, embodied, and expressed with reluctance. The prophet becomes a conduit of endurance. His gestures—scroll-eating, lying on his side, dumbness— signal that language has limits. Prophecy must sometimes speak through the body when the voice no longer suffices.

Ezekiel does not merely aim to transmit a divine message; he reshapes the receiver. The scroll serves a pedagogical purpose—not simply to convey information, but to prepare a community capable of embodying divine presence after exile. This preparation entails more than persuasion; it requires the deliberate dismantling of theological constructs inherited from the old world—temple permanence, prophetic reciprocity, and covenantal security. In their place, the scroll initiates a disciplined process of restraint, withdrawal, and emptying. These acts are not ends in themselves, but necessary ruptures in service of a larger purpose: to make space for a new creation of people, land, temple, and city—rebuilt not through restoration, but through transformation.

Teaching this book provides an opportunity to rethink communication, pedagogy, and theological agency. Use role-play to perform Ezekiel's communicative sequence, assigning students to play the roles of Sender, Prophet, and Shadowed Audience, who are limited in direct communication. The exercise reveals the dissonance built into the scroll's very structure.

• Introduce communication theory (Austin, Searle) to illustrate how prophetic speech in Ezekiel functions not as illocutionary persuasion but as archival inscription.

• Facilitate spatial and temporal mapping: trace how messages cross space (Babylon–Jerusalem) and time (present–future), identifying the prophetic cost of deferred hope.

Ezekiel challenges the preacher not to deliver results but to hold the burden. The preacher, like Ezekiel, may speak knowing that no one listens. Yet this does not invalidate the message—it affirms it.

Preaching from Ezekiel is not a proclamation for persuasion, but a speech for memory. The pulpit would become a site of holy endurance, not rhetorical control. The goal is not to generate a response but to witness faithfully— to hold open the space where divine words may echo even long after the sanctuary is empty.

Ezekiel's prophetic model does not assume closure. His scroll is a witness—not to a fulfilled mission, but to a preserved calling. Prophets do not succeed by changing their audience; they endure by bearing the Word. Ezekiel teaches us that deferred communication is not a divine failure, but rather divine patience for the greater purpose, and that speech, even if unanswered, can still be holy.

Conclusion to Part I

Early chapters of the Book of Ezekiel do not offer comfort or clarity. They offer rupture, demanding that readers prepare ethically with patience. What is missing — dialogue, intimacy, intercession — is as formative as what is present — symbol, silence, spectacle.

Part I has thus laid the interpretive groundwork: first by exploring what Ezekiel lacks and overflows with (Chapter 1), then how it has been received (Chapter 2), and finally how readers today are summoned to participate in its unfinished communication (Chapter 3). The following section will shift focus from the tensions and silences that frame Ezekiel's prophetic world to the compositional strategies and structural patterns that shape its theological messages. The scroll will move forward, but not by erasing its past: the gaps and excesses in its voice remain part of its theological architecture. The readings that follow will attend to these movements — of speech, gesture, and presence — as the scroll's performative architecture unfolds across its central visions and rhetorical acts. What unfolds next is not a resolution, but a closer tracing of these movements — where the book's architecture itself becomes a mode of prophetic speech.

Part II
Architecture and Voice — How Ezekiel Speaks

If Part I surveyed the asymmetries, silences, and disruptions that frame Ezekiel's prophetic vocation — what is not said, who does not listen, and how divine agency insists nonetheless — then Part II turns toward the scroll's compositional dynamism: how it is shaped to move, to act, and ultimately to speak with theological force.

Far from a disjointed archive of visions and oracles, the Book of Ezekiel unfolds with rigorous architectural intentionality. The structure of the book is not a neutral container; it is a theological argument. It moves rhythmically — through judgment, transition, and tentative restoration — not simply as a literary pattern but as a prophetic strategy. Each layer of the text contributes to a dramatic re-narration of Israel's history, not to reassert tradition but to interrupt it.

Unlike other prophetic texts that diagnose covenantal failure only to repeat cycles of repentance and relapse, Ezekiel goes further: it seeks to sever that pattern entirely. The book does not merely announce judgment and envision recovery. It interrogates the theological mechanisms that allowed Israel's history to fall into ritualized dysfunction — shallow remorse, temporary reform, relapse — and attempts to re-script covenantal identity from within the trauma of exile. The book presses toward a restoration that is not only future-facing but structurally and spiritually sustainable.

In this light, Part II approaches the Book of Ezekiel not only as a vessel of divine speech but as a compositional intelligence where sign-acts, lamentations, vision sequences, and judgment poetry function as deliberately arranged instruments of theological reconstruction. The prophet's body, silenced and scripted, becomes the medium not just for what God says, but for how God refrains from saying certain things too soon.

Three central sets of questions guide this section:

(1) What literary structures shape the Book of Ezekiel? How do macrostructures and internal literary symmetries organize and deepen the theological messages of the book?

(2) How do key passages serve as structural and theological hinges? What is at stake when pivotal texts such as chapters 10, 24, 33, and 37 disrupt existing rhetorical momentum or shift prophetic tone?

(3) How does Ezekiel re-narrate Israel's theological history to break its recursive pathology? What kinds of historical memory and covenantal imagination does the book sever, reweave, or elevate — and how do these dynamics shape a new vision of communal identity and divine presence?

Part II opens with a structural investigation in Chapter 4, exploring how the book's literary architecture signals and stages its theological priorities. Chapter 5 then analyzes selected passages that exemplify genre intensity, performativity, and thematic functions.

Together, these chapters guide the reader from an aerial perspective to ground-level engagement, tracing how the form of Ezekiel becomes its voice.

In Ezekiel, structure transcends mere scaffolding; it communicates theology. Form is not passive; it speaks, wounds, and at times offers hope.

Chapter 4
Understanding the Structures of the Book of Ezekiel
Toward a Communicative Architecture of Prophecy

To read the Book of Ezekiel is to experience disruption — not only in content but in form. The book resists linear development, proceeding through storm-chariot theophanies, embodied parables, legal disputations, and temple blueprints with little narrative continuity or closure. While chapters 1–24 reflect the inter-siege period between 597 and 586 BCE, the book continues beyond the destruction of Jerusalem, culminating in a vision dated fourteen years after its fall. In essence, while Ezekiel appears to present a chronological sequence — with its oracles indicated by dated superscriptions — the implied literary contexts of each passage are, overall, less sequential than they seem. Instead, the marked dates serve as literary and theological markers, preserving divine communication amidst fragmented time and disrupted narrative flow.

Communicative Mapping: Four Axes of Prophetic Discourse

A communicative model helps clarify the structure of the Book — not only by genre or date, but by mapping relationships between:

• Sender (YHWH): The divine voice, commanding but often withheld.

• Messenger (Ezekiel/"Son of Man"): A reticent performer rather than a persuasive orator.

• Receiver (Exiles and Jerusalemites): Split, deferred, and mostly unresponsive.

• Narrator (First-person Ezekiel): Temporally anchored but often suspended in a prophetic "present."

This mapping reveals a structure marked not by symmetry, but by misalignment—communication is often incomplete, its effects are delayed, and its intentions are preserved rather than enacted. Here are more detailed illustrations.

Ezekiel's Communicative Structure: Divine Speech and the Withheld Audience

The Book of Ezekiel is structured around an intricate communication system—layered, delayed, and often asymmetrical. While divine speech saturates the scroll, its recipients remain strangely silent or undefined. Commands are frequent, but confirmations are rare. What emerges is a prophetic drama that unfolds not through interpersonal dialogue but through restraint, abstraction, and preserved intensity.

YHWH the Sender: Speech Without Interlocutors

Throughout the book, YHWH speaks consistently—often at great length and with precise detail—but exclusively to Ezekiel. There is no recorded moment of direct divine-human conversation beyond this prophetic channel. Even urgent oracles of judgment are voiced without visible feedback loops, and YHWH repeatedly acknowledges the people's refusal or incapacity to hear (2:5; 3:7). Divine speech is not absent, but inaccessible.

More striking, however, is YHWH's deep investment in remaining withheld. The God of Ezekiel does not simply pronounce judgment; He withholds His own compassion. In contrast to Isaiah's God, who returns in mercy, or Jeremiah's God, who breaks into grief, Ezekiel's God restrains—even His tenderness. This restraint should not be mistaken for indifference. Instead, it reflects a purposeful refusal to console prematurely—a divine strategy to avoid sabotaging the more profound transformation required. YHWH's silence is not passive; it is charged with theological intention, resisting the temptation to comfort too soon. He withholds not to abandon but to prepare—for a creation that must emerge only after devastation has done its necessary work.

Ezekiel the Messenger: Obedient but Silenced

Ezekiel functions as a messenger, yet his role is marked more by reception than transmission. He is commanded to speak and act, but the text rarely confirms his fulfillment of those commands. Symbolic gestures such as the siege enactment (ch. 4) or exile reenactment (ch. 12) are described, but not narrated as performed. Others, like the death of his wife (ch. 24), are both enacted and interpreted. This uneven record reveals that Ezekiel's prophetic activity is not intended to model execution, but to script theological imagination.

Furthermore, Ezekiel's muteness (3:26) and physical restraint (4:8) suggest that even where communication is commanded, it is often delayed, diverted, or symbolically impaired. He is a prophet called to speak but withheld from speech. What we receive is not a transcript of action, but a scroll of deferred performance—intended not for immediate response, but for future recognition. In this way, Ezekiel's task is not to compel change, but to preserve meaning in a form that will survive the collapse of immediate hearing.

Receivers: Gaps, Glimpses, and Vanishing Addressees

Ezekiel resides among the exiles (3:15), yet most oracles in chapters 1–24 are directed toward those still in Jerusalem. While elders sometimes come to him (8:1; 14:1; 20:1), the broader community remains largely silent. The scroll contains no sustained narrative of response, no communal repentance, and few interpersonal exchanges.

Only three passages explicitly depict prophetic communication reaching the people:

• In 11:25, Ezekiel reports his vision to the elders, implying some level of reception.

• In 12:9, the people witness a symbolic act and ask, "What are you doing?" YHWH quotes their question and provides an interpretation through Ezekiel. Yet their voice is reframed, not directly recorded.

• In 24:24–27, the people respond to the prophet's sudden (restrictive) bereavement, ask its meaning, and receive an explanation. This remains the only unambiguous feedback loop—divine message, prophetic mediation, and communal response.

After the fall of Jerusalem, Ezekiel's voice is restored (33:22). Yet even then, narrative silence resumes. The subsequent oracles of restoration are not described as received or enacted. Most notably, the temple vision in chapters 40–48 — introduced with a command to "declare all this to the house of Israel" (40:4) — concludes with no visible audience. The city is measured. The gates are named. But no human ear is present. The implied reader is left to inherit the message.

This progressive evaporation of the audience challenges conventional assumptions about prophetic communication. Ezekiel is not a book of persuasion.

It is a sealed scroll, waiting to be opened by those yet capable of hearing.

Narrative Time and Theological Delay

Ezekiel is unusually saturated with date formulas, often recording the year, month, and day of divine encounters (e.g., 1:1–2; 8:1; 20:1; 24:1; 33:21; 40:1). These time-stamps function not to move the plot forward, but to mark the passage of revelation in suspended time. Communication unfolds in vision, not in dialogue, in symbolic performance, not in event resolution.

In exile, Ezekiel's community inhabits a temporality where dates are marked but not lived. The cyclical rhythms of pilgrimage festivals and covenantal gatherings are absent. In such a vacuum, the prophet's precision takes on a different register. These notations resemble less a liturgical calendar than a survival strategy — like Robinson Crusoe tallying days after shipwreck, Ezekiel marks time as an act of resistance against historical erasure. This scroll is not reacting to crisis; instead, it archives divine presence for a future that can receive it.

The final date marker in 40:1 occurs fourteen years after the city's fall. As mentioned above, what follows is not a message of immediate restoration, but a carefully drawn vision whose delivery remains undocumented. This theological withholding reinforces the scroll's enduring structure: what is spoken is preserved, not necessarily received.

In sum, Ezekiel's communicative architecture enacts what it proclaims: divine speech may be fully voiced, but until the hearer meets certain circumstances, like the fall of the nation, the messages would remain mostly suspended. YHWH speaks not to provoke immediate repentance and immediate restoration, but to initiate a long work of re-creation. The prophet does not merely transmit content; he participates in a process of unbuilding—a strategic dismantling of inherited assumptions about temple, covenant, and communication. Only then can a new creation—of people, city, land, and temple—emerge, not as restoration of the old, but as transformation toward the enduring.

Even if the book concludes without a specific human addressee, it still engages a reader. The absence of an audience within the narrative allows for the reader to enter, not just as an observer, but as the very person being addressed. The Book of Ezekiel is perhaps preserved not for its original audience but for those capable of receiving it after the collapse of direct communication. Its delayed reception invites the reader into a dual task: to reconstruct meaning out of theological fragments, and to respond—not with reactive emotion, but with enduring attentiveness. The final question is not whether the people listened then, but whether the reader will listen now.

Structures of Silence and Intensity

Rather than progressing in a smooth arc from judgment to restoration, the Book of Ezekiel unfolds in pulses: visionary openings (ch. 1), silences and muting (ch. 3), extended judgment oracles (chs. 4–24), abrupt shifts to hope (chs. 33–39), and finally, meticulously measured visions of a renewed sanctuary and land (chs. 40–48). These sections do not resolve what came before; instead, they intensify the instability of divine presence and human responsibility.

The book's structure performs what its content narrates: rupture, withdrawal, return, and unpredictability. Key hinge chapters—10, 24, 33, and 37—do not serve as smooth transitions but function as theological ruptures. They arrest rhetorical flow and demand ethical and liturgical reconsideration. These are thresholds, not conclusions.

Structural Tropes: When Architecture Becomes Theology

The architecture of Ezekiel—both literary and spatial—is itself theological. Its structural devices are not merely ornamental, but performative:

• Opening and Closing Visions (ch. 1 and chs. 40–48): From mobile glory to static measurements—a movement from divine approach to divine delineation.

• Repeated Refrains ("Then they shall know that I am YHWH" / "My eye will not pity, nor will I spare"): Divine Self-Refrain — not a closure, but a refrain of deferred recognition, echoing YHWH's own unyielding stance of judgment and mercy withheld.

In this way, the book functions as a kind of textual sanctuary. It opens with divine presence in exile and ends with a mapped vision of reordered space. This is not simply literary artistry; it is liturgical choreography. The scroll does not resolve trauma—it spatializes it, preserving divine intent through form.

Unlike the interactive prophetic engagements in Isaiah (with kings) or the emotional dialogue of Jeremiah (with God), Ezekiel's prophecy refuses immediacy. His speech is framed by divine discretion, as stated in Ezekiel 3:26–27, "I will make your tongue stick to the roof of your mouth... but when I speak with you, I will open your mouth." This controlled speech act signals a shift from real-time persuasion to archival prophecy—designed not to elicit immediate repentance, but to survive judgment.

Ezekiel thus emerges as a prophet without a live audience, yet with a theologically charged silence. His enforced muteness is not a flaw, but a strategy. It transforms the scroll into a repository of deferred meaning—an archive-in-motion awaiting future encounter.

And this introduces a crucial addition to the communicative schema: the reader. Where speech failed to reach the original audience, it now addresses the reader directly, not as a neutral spectator, but as an inheritor of the scroll's burden and possibility. Interpretation becomes the act of answering a message once it is suspended. The reader becomes the new participant in a drama that was never closed.

In the Classroom: Visualizing Theological Form

This chapter invites pedagogical approaches that draw attention to form as content.

Structural Mapping Exercise: Have students trace the book's rhetorical flow across its three major units (judgment, transition, restoration), noting where transitions falter or implode.

Audience Reconstruction: Assign small groups to map rhetorical direction—who is addressed, who hears, who responds? How does this change between chapters 4, 12, and 33?

Preaching Insights: When Form Refuses Closure

To preach Ezekiel is to preach from within an unfinished structure. The scroll teaches us that divine speech is not always linear or persuasive—it may instead be preserved, staged, or measured. The preacher stands not as an interpreter of resolved meaning but as a witness to sacred design in process.

Ezekiel models a homiletic of construction without arrival. His scroll ends not with communal restoration but with divine presence named—YHWH *Shammah*.

This is a preaching not of solution, but of sacred scaffolding: trust built upon silence, design drawn in exile, and hope measured in uninhabited space.

Chapter 5
Reading Ezekiel Passage by Passage

Building on the previous chapters' exploration of theological displacement and fractured audience dynamics, this chapter reads Ezekiel passage by passage to honor the tension, delay, and theological urgency built into its architecture.

Ezekiel does not communicate with a responsive community. His prophetic world is not dialogical, but custodial. Divine words are spoken, not to be received in real-time, but to be recorded, preserved, and eventually remembered. What might appear as rhetorical dislocation is, in fact, a deliberate theological strategy: a deferred communication that protects the scroll's authority from the instability of its human recipients.

This chapter not only highlights the theme of delay but also explores why such a postponement is so crucial. It offers a compelling response based on the covenantal principles outlined in Leviticus 26, which are central to the H tradition. Leviticus 26 describes the journey from exile to restoration not as a sudden return but as a process involving moral reflection, collective confession, and divine remembrance. The Book of Ezekiel adapts this theology to fit his own context. Exile is already a reality; thus, the pressing question is no longer when restoration will occur, but rather how people prevent falling into despair once more.

Hence, in Chapter 5, we read Ezekiel's passages not only as traumatic responses but as blueprints for resilience. The Book of Ezekiel is filled with architectural visions, behavioral constraints, and spatial redesigns— intended not to celebrate a return to the past, but to safeguard the future. The scroll becomes the small and temporary sanctuary YHWH promised in 11:16—not a place of worship, but a memory palace of sanctity designed to resist relapse.

To guide close engagement with each unit of Ezekiel, this chapter follows a recurring structure across passages: *Literary Time, Communicative Flow, Symbols and Keywords, Form and Genre, Thematic Functions, In the Classroom,* and *Preaching Insights.* This framework allows both literary nuance and theological resonance to surface—inviting academic analysis alongside pedagogical and pastoral application.

Ezekiel 1–3: Prophecy Without Response

Ezekiel 1–3 opens with cosmic rupture. The prophet does not plead or protest; he beholds. In a storm-chariot theophany, divine presence erupts into exile—not to comfort the displaced but to conscript a messenger into a mission of deferred reception. These chapters form a threshold— not only for Ezekiel's ministry but for the reader's interpretive orientation. From the outset, the book subverts expectations of prophecy as a dialogue, proposing instead a vision-centered, body-mediated, and text-preserving vocation.

Literary Time

Ezekiel's visions do not unfold in linear time. Instead, they form a web of theological disclosure where meaning is often withheld, rearranged, or revealed retrospectively. This is not merely a function of chronology, but a literary strategy of deferred recognition—one that demands the reader's participation in reconstructing the order of divine communication.

A key example appears in the opening vision of Ezekiel 1. There, the prophet encounters a shocking theophany: a storm, a fiery cloud, and the divine throne borne by hybrid living creatures, descending not upon Zion but by the Chebar canal. This mobile throne—emphatically glorious, yet spatially dislocated—appears without explanation. No contextual rationale is given for why the divine glory has left its expected location. The vision explodes into view, but its meaning remains suspended.

Only a year later, in Ezekiel 8–11, the narrative returns to Jerusalem. In this vision, dated to the sixth year from the beginning of exile (cf. 8:1), the mystery begins to resolve. Within the temple itself, the prophet witnesses idolatrous rites, corrupt leadership, and escalating abominations. Ezekiel 10 describes the very throne from Ezekiel 1 now lifting from the Holy of Holies and departing eastward. What once descended into mystery is now seen in motion: not a random eruption, but a response to covenantal violation.

In this way, the divine theophany of Ezekiel 1 receives its interpretive context only after the fact. What initially appears as unannounced glory becomes retroactively intelligible as divine withdrawal. The text thus performs a kind of theological retrospection, asking the reader to return to the earlier vision and reinterpret it in light of what is later disclosed. Revelation in Ezekiel is not merely sequential; it is recursive.

In sum, the time structure of Ezekiel does not guide the reader gently through stages of understanding. It shocks first, explains later. The vision of Ezekiel 1 functions not as an introduction, but as a provocation—its theological coherence withheld until the retrospective logic of chapters 8–11 recontextualizes divine mobility as judgmental departure. It is through this disjunctive rhythm—divine presence first, temple abandonment second—that the scroll teaches its audience not just what God does, but how divine meaning must be patiently discerned. What is first seen in glory must be re-seen in grief. What erupts in vision must be endured in silence before it is understood in narrative.

Communicative Flow

God speaks—but not to Israel. The opening sequence is structured with a vertical axis: the divine voice descends, the prophet is taken hold of, yet no one else hears. YHWH commissions Ezekiel, warns him of the hardened hearts he will encounter, and preemptively silences him (3:26). This approach is not one of persuasion; rather, it embodies a theology of estrangement. Communication exists, but it is misaligned—YHWH to Ezekiel, then Ezekiel to a future audience, with meaning that is yet to unfold. The scroll is not intended to change minds, but rather to serve as a preserved witness.

Form and Genre

The literary composition of Ezekiel 1-3 manifests a complex interplay of distinct genres, notably encompassing a throne vision (ch. 1), a commission narrative (chs. 2 and 3), and an element of ritual silence (ch. 3). This multifaceted genre blending not only enriches the theological depth of the text but also underscores the prophet's unique role and the nature of his divine mandate. Ezekiel's encounter mirrors Isaiah's temple vision and Jeremiah's call, but its sensory scale is unmatched. The scroll-vision is literary hybridity at its peak—combining priestly liturgy, apocalyptic symbology, and prophetic dread. Ezekiel is less an active agent than a vessel, overwhelmed and animated by divine presence.

Symbols and Keywords

The chariot (*merkavah*) in Ezekiel 1 is not a vehicle of transportation but a mobile throne, representing divine sovereignty, mobility, and cosmic control. It descends rather than ascends, marking divine initiative and disruptive presence. Instead of conforming to anthropocentric geometry, the divine mobility displays non-linearity, simultaneity, and multidirectional propulsion—resisting any singular frame of motion or meaning. The merkavah's composite structure evokes mystery: its throne-like form renders YHWH not simply as one who sits, but as one enthroned in motion—ruling while moving, sovereign yet uncontained.

The wheels "full of eyes [*'eynayim*] all around" (1:18) symbolize divine omniscience as well as function as an anticipatory mirror of Ezekiel's own prophetic vocation. The prophet must not merely see but become seeing—become vigilance embodied. The proliferation of eyes destabilizes any notion of fixed surveillance; instead, vision operates in an all-encompassing mode, rendering the prophet ethically and perceptually accountable.

The scroll (*megillah*) Ezekiel receives (2:9– 3:3) is both sweet as honey and filled with "lamentation and mourning and woe" (2:10). It is to be consumed, not proclaimed—an internalized text that paradoxically prepares the prophet for speech by first silencing him. The scroll is therefore a performative paradox: it contains speech but speaks only through digestion; it is read inwardly, not aloud. This points to a theology of embodied revelation, where the divine word must become prophetic flesh.

45

Already from its opening vision, the Book of Ezekiel presents divine presence through contradictory metaphors — commanding yet withdrawn, intimate yet unapproachable. What might appear as syntactic or grammatical inconsistency is, in fact, a sign of the text's resistance to stable anthropomorphic representation. This refusal begins already in the inaugural theophany, where linguistic structures themselves resist binary assignment.

In Ezekiel 1-2, grammatical mismatches emerge: feminine subjects are paired with masculine verbs, or vice versa. These are not errors; they are linguistic signals of a theological excess. Like fire and ice coexisting without canceling each other or living creatures moving without turning while the wheels move in any of four directions (1:12, 1:17), the divine presence is rendered through paradox. It is simultaneously directional and undirected, mobile and enthroned, commanding yet silent. Ezekiel's own calling mirrors this tension — he is told to "proclaim" and "shut down the door" at once, to remain fixed as a sentinel while moving with the spirit. These contradictions are not flaws but essential features of the vision, dramatizing a reality that exceeds human dimensionality.

The text invites us, then, to consider this as intentional disorientation. Just as three-dimensional space resists full representation in two dimensions, the divine glory, what Ezekiel calls "the appearance of the likeness of the glory of YHWH," is described through layered, unstable images. These are not simply metaphors; they are attempts to trace a presence that overflows language, gender, and space. The result is not theological incoherence, but a form of revelation that reveals by rupturing. The prophet does not master the vision; he is undone by it, becoming its vessel rather than its interpreter.

Thematic Functions

Holiness takes on a dynamic quality; speech becomes unyielding. Instead of focusing on mission-driven prophecy, Ezekiel 1-3 introduces vocation without expecting a response from the audience. YHWH asserts clearly: "they will not listen... but they shall know that a prophet has been among them" (2:5, 3:7). This declaration redefines prophetic success as the discernible presence of the divine, even in the face of rejection, rather than simply leading people's repentance. The people's silence is, therefore, not indicative of failure. Prophecy transforms into evidence rather than argument; it embodies presence instead of persuasion.

In the Classroom

This passage presents rich opportunities for implementing multisensory pedagogy:

Visual Theophany: Students can engage in a creative project by drawing or constructing a chariot, allowing them to explore and reflect on profound theological themes such as mobility, mystery, and divine sovereignty. This hands-on activity encourages them to visualize and internalize the abstract concepts in a tangible way.

Performance Silence: In a dynamic enactment, one student can voice the lines of YHWH, while another student embodies Ezekiel, maintaining a profound silence yet holding a scroll that signifies the weight of the prophetic message. This juxtaposition of speech and silence can deepen the understanding of the roles and relationships between the divine and the prophet.

Initiation Ritual: The prophet's deliberate seven-day silence (Ezekiel 3:15) can be interpreted as a symbolic representation of priestly liminality, echoing themes found in Leviticus 8:33. This framing positions Ezekiel not merely as a messenger but also as a ritually suspended intercessor, highlighting the complexities of his role within the sacred narrative. This exploration invites students to consider the transformative power of silence and the deeper spiritual implications of Ezekiel's experience.

Preaching Insights

Ezekiel's call begins not in the temple, but in the land of forced displacement. YHWH appears not in Zion but by the Chebar canal—an unclean place among the exiles. This is the first scandal: that the glory of God descends not upon the throne in Jerusalem, but among the deported, on foreign soil. For the modern preacher, this poses a radical challenge: can we trust divine presence in the places we were taught to expect absence?

Ezekiel is called not as a public speaker but as a stunned watcher—immobilized by vision, overrun by glory, and silenced by command. He is appointed a prophet at the very moment his mouth is shut. He is to speak to people who will not hear, and yet he is commanded to ingest the scroll. The prophetic task, then, begins not with words but with embodied digestion, with the internalization of judgment and lamentation.

Ezekiel 1–3 reframes preaching not as persuasive proclamation, but as faithful displacement. The preacher is not immediately sent to proclaim, but first to be undone, to sit where the exiles sit (cf. 3:15), and to bear the weight of a message no one may believe. In this space, ministry becomes not a performance of answers, but a stewardship of divine strangeness — a willingness to be saturated in the Word before ever speaking it.

To preach Ezekiel is to enter a space of theological delay: trusting that the scroll will be opened in time, that silence is not the absence of vocation, but its gestational form. The urgency of the prophet is not measured by volume, but by presence. In Ezekiel 1–3, we are invited to consider that divine calling may begin in exile, remain unanswered, and still be holy.

Ezekiel 4–7: Road to the End

Ezekiel 4-7 marks the prophet's first recorded reception of divine command for public action. Yet notably, the text remains silent as to whether these performances were executed or how they were received. Therefore, instead of genuine public engagement, Ezekiel 4–7 illustrates the assigned act of prophecy — reporting divine intent rather than delivering it.

Literary Time

Unlike Ezekiel 1–3, this unit lacks explicit date formulas, creating a moment of temporal suspension. Yet because it immediately follows the dated inaugural vision (1:1–3:15), the prophetic actions in Ezekiel 4–7 are implicitly situated within the same early season of Ezekiel's ministry. The absence of new dates signals a kind of frozen prophetic time — a sustained present in which the earliest judgments begin to take visible shape, but without narrative movement. The weight of divine warning intensifies but does not yet resolve.

This temporal suspension serves as a literary function: it generates pressure. Ezekiel 4–7 does not simply continue the inaugural commission; it escalates it. The prophet's dramatic sign-acts, oracles of doom, and catalogues of national collapse all lead toward a narrative and theological crescendo—one that will break open in the visionary detonation of Ezekiel 8–11. In that later unit, Ezekiel is transported to Jerusalem, where the source of divine wrath is finally exposed: abominations in the temple, corruption among the leaders, and the shocking departure of YHWH's glory.

From the reader's perspective, Ezekiel 4–7 operates like the tightening coil of a narrative spring. The text builds tension through intensification. It climbs toward a silent apex, preparing the way for the explosive vision in Ezekiel 9, where judgment begins, and Ezekiel 10, where the throne-chariot is seen departing the temple. Thus, even though these chapters are not visionary in genre, they serve as the theological runway for what follows.

In terms of literary time, Ezekiel 4–7 functions as the quiet before the storm—quiet only in structure, not in tone. Their undated status conceals their urgency, even as they carry the scroll's earliest enacted judgment toward its climactic unveiling. The result is a unit that feels suspended yet thick with movement, pressing forward not with speed, but with weight.

Communicative Flow

Ezekiel's prophetic commission unfolds through a series of asymmetrical exchanges between YHWH and the prophet—what may be called communication without reply, and yet not without communion.

In Ezekiel 4–5, YHWH issues a series of precise, performative commands: construct a miniature siege scene using brick and iron (4:1–3); lie on his left and right sides for an exact number of days (4:4–8); eat rationed bread cooked initially over human dung (4:9–17); and shave his head and divide the hair by fire, sword, and scattering, reserving only a few strands (5:1-4).

These gestures are not merely symbolic; they are communicative acts that encode divine judgment onto the prophet's body. They dramatize siege, starvation, shame, and exile. Yet there is no mention of an audience. The performance is given but not received—at least not visibly. Ezekiel becomes both messenger and message, a silent bearer of divine fury staged before an absent or unresponsive public.

And yet, communication is not one-directional. In 4:14, Ezekiel interrupts, "Ah, Lord YHWH! Behold, I have never defiled myself..." This brief protest— concerning the cooking fuel—reminds the reader that the prophet is not a mute puppet. He resists. He modifies. And remarkably, YHWH relents, substituting cow dung for human waste (4:15). This moment, however brief, reveals that divine communication in exile includes negotiation. The theater is not empty of voice—it contains struggle.

Ezekiel 6-7 shifts dramatically in tone and form. The prophet disappears as a character, and YHWH's voice dominates the stage: "They shall know that I am YHWH." (6:7, 10, 13, etc.)

The language becomes oracular and reiterative, filled with refrains of divine recognition, judgment, and destruction. These monologues are marked by rhetorical intensity and literary closure, yet again—no explicit human audience is shown responding. Communication here becomes saturated but unreceived, a divine soliloquy echoing into the ruins.

Together, Ezekiel 4-7 presents a prophetic mode in which communication is enacted, not assumed. It is performative, contested, and often unilateral. Ezekiel's protest in chapter 4, the tactile ritual of hair division in chapter 5, and the unrelenting declarations in chapters 6–7 all attest to a theological world in which the Word moves — even if no one hears.

Form and Genre
The passage blends symbolic action and spoken oracle: Sign-acts dominate chapters 4–5, such as the brick siege, body posture, and ritual defilement. Oracular forms re-emerge in chapters 6–7, including covenant lawsuits (6:1–10) and dirges (7:1–27). This hybrid structure blurs boundaries between prophecy and theater, where judgment is rehearsed as much as proclaimed.

Symbols and Keywords
Ezekiel 4–5 deploys a series of embodied signs that function as symbolic enactments of national judgment. Each act resonates with covenantal imagery and contributes to a cumulative portrait of disintegration.

The prophet is first instructed to draw Jerusalem on a brick and place an iron pan between himself and the city (4:1–3), signifying both the impending siege and the divine impenetrability that now separates YHWH from the people. He then lies on his side — 390 days for Israel and 40 for Judah (4:4–8) — visually bearing the duration of each kingdom's guilt. The rationed bread and impure fuel (4:9–15) dramatize the extreme scarcity and ritual defilement of exile. Finally, in a sharp gesture of covenantal fragmentation, Ezekiel cuts his hair with a sword, dividing it into thirds: one burned, one scattered, and one kept briefly before even that is cast into fire (5:1–4). Each movement of the prophet's body becomes a prophetic text in itself.

These signs are not arbitrary. They echo the covenantal warnings of Leviticus 26 and Deuteronomy 28, where disobedience leads to famine, defeat, desecration, and exile. In Ezekiel's performance, the body becomes a stage upon which the national collapse is foretold — not merely described but enacted.

Thematic Functions

Through Ezekiel's immobilized body and disfiguring tasks, YHWH communicates the irreversible cost of covenantal abandonment. The symbolic acts are not illustrative but destructive performances, designed to sever the exilic audience's residual nostalgia for Jerusalem.

The fate of the prophet's hair in 5:1-4 — burned, struck, scattered, and a remnant thrown into fire — reflects more than political disintegration. It signals theological despair: even the spared are consumed. There is no clean category of "survivor." By turning Ezekiel into both a sign and a site of devastation, the text disorients hopes of restoration or remnant security in the near future.

This disorientation sharpens into finality in Ezekiel 7. There, the repeated declaration "An end has come... the end has come" (7:2-6) functions as a liturgical anti-climax, countering any expectation that this judgment is a mere episode. The rhetoric announces not cyclical punishment but irreversible closure — a theological severance with no return ticket. Unlike earlier prophetic cycles where destruction folds into hope, here the refrain intensifies: "The end has come" is not a transition — it is the finale.

In Ezekiel 4-7, divine wrath does not invite resolution but demands reckoning. The prophet is made to embody this reckoning — paralyzed, starved, and shaved — not to restore memory, but to cancel sentimental memory altogether.

In the Classroom

Invite students to map Ezekiel's symbolic acts within the timeline from Ezekiel's deportation to Jerusalem's fall (597-586 BCE). When did the siege begin? When was the temple destroyed? How does the duration of Ezekiel's lying down intersect with these national traumas?

Assign roles for a dramatic reading: YHWH, Ezekiel, and a silent observing crowd. Encourage students to notice the imbalance of power and voice: Who speaks? Who listens? Who reacts? Let the silence of the "audience" become a space of interpretive tension rather than absence.

Guide students to interpret each action as a theological proposition. What does it mean to eat rationed food while using dung as fuel? What emotions arise in performing judgment without response?

Assign each student the role of a strand of Ezekiel's hair (cf. 5:1-4): one to be burned, one struck with a sword, one scattered to the wind, one hidden in the folds of the robe, one later thrown into the fire. Invite them to speak or write from that position: What does it feel like to be spared but still endangered? What does judgment feel like when it does not distinguish? What happens when you are part of a remnant now, only to be cast back into destruction soon?

This embodied exercise allows students to confront the theological ambiguity of Ezekiel's actions — not merely interpreting them as symbols but inhabiting their disorientation. Teaching Ezekiel 4–7 through dramatic and empathic entry opens space for theological reckoning and prophetic imagination in exile.

Preaching Insights

Ezekiel 4-7 confronts preachers with a paradox: how does one proclaim a message of "the end" without surrendering to despair? Chapter 7's refrain—"An end has come, the end has come upon the four corners of the land" (7:2)—is liturgically stark and theologically final. Yet preaching from this passage does not require pronouncing hopelessness. Rather, it demands a courageous homiletic transformation: to name the end in such a way that it prepares for something holy to begin.

For Ezekiel, "the end" is not merely chronological but theological. It signals the collapse of illusions—false hope, misplaced nostalgia, and inherited entitlement. That collapse clears space not for cheap comfort, but for truthful reckoning. The preacher today is called into similar spaces of spiritual apathy and cultural denial, speaking with a voice that cuts through resistance—not to dominate, but to awaken.

This preaching does not hinge on persuasion but on faithful embodiment of divine reality. The scroll may not be received by the audience now—but it must be digested by the preacher nonetheless. Proclaiming Ezekiel 4-7 means daring to say that God has ended what must not continue—idolatry, denial, betrayal—so that covenant renewal might arise not from memory, but from fire.

In this task, Ezekiel 6:9 offers a profound theological anchor. There, God declares that the people's adulterous eyes and hearts will be shattered—but also says, "I was broken by their whoring heart." This moment reframes divine judgment: not as detached violence, but as a divine rupture from within. YHWH does not crush from above but breaks from within, bearing pain for the sake of a greater purpose.

To preach from Ezekiel 4–7, then, is to make space for that shared brokenness—to invite the community into the recognition that divine judgment is not God's emotional absence, but God's costly presence. And if the preacher can name this, and help the hearers linger there, then the sermon has already begun—even in silence, even before response.

Ezekiel 8–11: Seeing What Must Leave

Chapters 8–11 form a tightly woven vision sequence, one of the most theologically charged segments in the book of Ezekiel. It portrays the horrifying reality that YHWH's glory—once enthroned in the Jerusalem temple—has begun to leave. The prophet, in exile, is transported in a vision to Jerusalem, where he witnesses a multi-layered infiltration of idolatry within the temple precincts, culminating in the divine decision to vacate the sanctuary.

Literary Time

Following the undated intensity of chapters 4–7, the vision in Ezekiel 8–11 is re-anchored to a precise time stamp: "the sixth year, in the sixth month, on the fifth day" (8:1).

This vision is dated to the sixth year (591 BCE), just over a year after Ezekiel's inaugural vision (592 BCE), and situated between the first deportation (597 BCE) and the eventual fall of Jerusalem (586 BCE). The moment is geopolitically charged: Judah, under pressure from both Babylon and Egypt, faces rising internal instability and misplaced national hopes.

But literary time in Ezekiel is not simply chronological—it is theological. What appears in Ezekiel 8 as a newly timed vision is, in fact, a retrospective key. As mentioned above, it finally unveils the meaning of the throne-chariot's shocking descent in Ezekiel 1. The divine presence that once appeared inexplicably above the Chebar canal—mobile, radiant, and untethered—is now seen in motion again. But this time, it is not arriving. It is leaving.

Ezekiel 8–11 thus forms a hinge in the scroll's temporal architecture. After the tension-building stillness of Ezekiel 4–7, these chapters burst open with vision. Ezekiel is brought, perhaps more accurately, dragged, into the very heart of Jerusalem's temple, where he witnesses escalating abominations: secret chambers of idolatry, ritual violence, and corrupt leadership. Ezekiel 9 explodes in judgment, and Ezekiel 10 shows the glory of YHWH departing from the inner sanctuary. What began as an unspoken threat now becomes a visible rupture.

This is not a new beginning, but a delayed unveiling. The meaning of Ezekiel 1's theophany comes into focus only through the retrospective clarity of this unit. Literary time folds backward: the mobile throne that stunned the prophet at the start now reveals its logic. The reader is invited to reread, to reinterpret. The divine chariot is not simply transcendent—it is judicial. Its mobility is not random but responsive.

Ezekiel 8–11, then, is not only a visionary climax; it is a literary key. It retroactively reconfigures the scroll's earlier visions and establishes a new horizon of divine movement—away from the sacred center, into exile. The datedness of this vision reinforces its role: this is not timeless theology; it is a historically located rupture. And it leaves no room for delay. The temple is still standing, but its glory is beginning to fade.

Communicative Flow

The vision of Ezekiel 8–11 unfolds with a layered communicative structure that begins intimately and culminates expansively. YHWH is the ultimate sender of the message, initiating a visionary sequence that is both searing and revelatory. Ezekiel, as the prophetic messenger, functions not simply as a speaker but as a fully immersed visionary participant—his body and senses drawn into the divine indictment.

At first, the vision appears to be directed solely to Ezekiel, a private revelation unfolding while the elders of Judah are "sitting before" him (8:1). These elders act as narrative catalysts but remain visually passive; they do not witness what Ezekiel sees. This creates a marked interior-exterior dynamic: the prophet sees, absorbs, and processes what others do not—yet his eventual task is to relay it faithfully.

By the end of the sequence, in 11:25, Ezekiel does exactly that: he reports the entire vision to the exiles, extending its communicative reach from the solitary prophetic body to the dispersed communal body. The audience thus expands to include not only the initial elders in Babylon but the larger scattered exilic communities addressed in 11:16–21.

Within the vision itself, a further contrast is drawn between the inhabitants of Jerusalem. Some assert confidence in divine nearness, interpreting their continued presence in the land as evidence of chosenness. Others live under the shadow of perceived abandonment. Ezekiel's vision reframes these interpretations, suggesting that divine presence has in fact begun to relocate—not to the temple in Jerusalem, but toward the scattered and broken.

This reorientation is the heart of the communicative flow: though Ezekiel alone sees the glory departing the temple, the message is not private.

It is meant to prepare the exiles to receive a new theological geography — one that distinguishes between nostalgia and true hope, and one that ultimately centers God's restorative presence among the displaced.

Form and Genre

Ezekiel 8-11 is composed as a first-person visionary narrative, in which the prophet recounts his experience of being lifted "by the hair of his head" (8:3) and transported to Jerusalem. The genre is multi-layered, combining several prophetic and narrative forms. It opens as a vision report (8:1-3), then unfolds as a guided temple tour — not of sacred order, but of hidden desecration (8:5-16), contrasting sharply with the later idealized temple vision in Ezekiel 40-48. The unit escalates into a divine judgment narrative with angelic executioners (9:1-11), followed by a detailed glory movement account (10:1-22; 11:22-25), in which YHWH's presence departs the temple. The structure culminates in an oracle of conditional restoration (11:14-21), offering hope from exile. The cumulative effect is dramatic and disorienting, tracing a downward spiral — from revelation of abominations to divine abandonment — before opening a narrow path toward covenantal return. The genre thus mirrors the theological arc it narrates.

Symbols and Keywords

Ezekiel 8-11 builds its theological drama through a sequence of potent symbols, each deepening the narrative of desecration and divine withdrawal. It begins with the mysterious "image of jealousy" (8:3-5) — a totemic presence never fully explained, rendering it all the more threatening as a catalyst for divine offense. This is followed by a profusion of idolatrous imagery — creeping things and carved idols on the temple walls (8:10) — which visually saturate the space with impurity in stark contrast to Levitical codes. A more chilling image comes with seventy elders, including Jaazaniah (meaning "YHWH listens"), son of Shaphan, standing in a dark chamber holding censers (8:11). This combination evokes Numbers 16, where censers signal priestly rebellion and provoke divine judgment. There, censors become artifacts of warning; here, they become emblems of internal corruption. The elders' role is inverted — they are not intercessors but accomplices. Ezekiel 8 finishes by showing the sun worshippers turning their backs on the temple to worship the sun (8:16). Together, these desecrations dismantle the sanctuary from within.

In Ezekiel 9:2, six executioners and a seventh man "clothed in linen" arrive from the *north gate*, signaling both the Babylonian invasion and the priestly procedure. The linen-garbed figure, reminiscent of Levitical purity (cf. Lev 16:4), is not a warrior but a scribe. His task is sacred: to mark a *tav* (וָתּ) on the foreheads of those who mourn (9:4), echoing apotropaic traditions (cf. Exod 12:7) and revealing YHWH's mercy amid judgment. Judgment itself unfolds in priestly space. In 9:7, the executioners are told to defile the temple by filling it with the corpses of the slain — turning once-sacred space into a site of abomination. The very bodies of the judged become instruments of desecration.

In Chapter 11, Pelatiah (meaning "YHWH enables me to escape") unexpectedly dies during Ezekiel's vision (11:13). His death represents a dramatic manifestation of divine judgment impinging on the prophet's emotional state. As a representative leader, his fall signifies the symbolic collapse of the Jerusalem elite. Conversely, in 11:16, amidst the devastation, a glimmer of hope is offered specifically to the exiles rather than to the Jerusalemites: YHWH proclaims, "Though I have removed them far among the nations... I have become to them a *Miqdash Me'at* — a little sanctuary." This phrase redefines divine presence not as fixed in space, but as inherently relational and mobile. Even in exile, God grants a fragment of holiness — portable, concealed, and enduring.

Ultimately, YHWH's glory departs in stages — from the sanctuary to the gate and then to the Mount of Olives — mirroring the fragmentation of both the people and the priesthood.

Thematic Functions

Ezekiel 8-11 functions as a theologically inverted pilgrimage. Rather than ascending into divine presence, the prophet is led through desecration, witnessing the accumulated defilements that compel YHWH's departure. Divine wrath here is not impulsive but reluctantly enacted. The Glory departs not in haste but in stages — first from the inner sanctuary to the threshold (9:3), then to the east gate (10:18-19), and finally to the Mount of Olives (11:23). Holiness lingers, even as judgment proceeds.

Theologically, the section reframes exile not as abandonment but as the necessary result of divine withdrawal due to desecration. YHWH does not disappear; He relocates. In doing so, the locus of hope shifts — from Jerusalem to the exilic community. The conditional promise in 11:14-21, embedded within judgment, suggests that exile is not an erasure but a theological realignment — a displacement that makes future reconstitution possible.

In this light, the vision urges the exiles to sever nostalgia for Jerusalem. It declares that judgment must purify the land, while faith must be sustained in exile.

The call is twofold: to relinquish misplaced longing and to receive the "little sanctuary" (11:16) as a sign of enduring covenantal presence.

In the Classroom

This passage is ideal for visual mapping and spatial analysis. The complexity of Ezekiel's vision lends itself to embodied and imaginative classroom engagement:

Temple Map Exercise: Invite students to recreate Ezekiel's visionary journey through the temple (chapters 8–11), marking where each act of idolatry occurs. Discuss how the proximity to the Holy of Holies intensifies the gravity of the abominations and raises the stakes of divine response.

Glory Tracking: Chart the movement of YHWH's glory from the inner sanctuary (9:3) to the east gate (10:19) and finally to the Mount of Olives (11:23). Then revisit Ezekiel 1, where the throne appears above the Chebar canal. What theological or narrative logic explains this trajectory? Does the sequence suggest divine patience, sorrow, or reorientation?

Visualize the *Miqdash Me'at*: Ask students to imagine and construct what a "little sanctuary" (11:16) might look like in their own time and place. Where might such a space exist in exile? What form would divine presence take when the temple is no longer accessible?

Theological Roleplay: Assign students different roles—Ezekiel, the silent elders, the marked remnant, or the angelic executioners—and invite them to respond to the unfolding vision. What moral or theological tensions arise from each perspective? What is seen, what is withheld, and what is endured?

Preaching from Ezekiel 8–11 calls not only for interpreting a past vision, but for discerning how our current worship may mirror its distortions. The preacher is invited to zoom out — to ask whether we, too, have settled into sacred routines while unknowingly facing the wrong direction. Have we defined worship by form while turning our backs on presence?

The text warns that even the temple's innermost court can become a theater of misaligned devotion. What we justify in darkness may already be under divine surveillance. Thus, Ezekiel challenges us to name desecration not as distant or historical, but as potentially present and collective.

At the same time, for communities who feel exiled — cut off, overlooked, or forgotten — the temptation arises to interpret their displacement as abandonment. But the preacher must pause. Is exile a sign of divine rejection or divine relocation? Before answering for others, the preacher must first ask: How do I interpret God's movement in the spaces I call absence?

The preacher's task, then, is not to pronounce judgment, but to illuminate complexity. God's glory departs slowly. His grief precedes His absence. And even in exile, He prepares a sanctuary for those who mourn what was lost.

Ezekiel 12–23: Performed Judgment and Theological Dissonance

A heightened rhetorical intensity and significant theological volatility mark Ezekiel 12–23. These chapters encompass the precarious period between the Babylonian deportation of the Jehoiachin community (597 BCE) and the second siege of Jerusalem (588 BCE). Within this temporal and theological liminality, divine communication intensifies, while human response wanes. However, amidst the devastation of a city, we also witness a breakdown of communicative coherence. God speaks, Ezekiel acts, yet the people remain largely silent or filled with suspicion. This section presents striking personifications of Jerusalem (chs. 16, 23), alongside a rare but crucial discussion regarding generational guilt and moral agency (ch. 18).

Literary Time

Most of the chapters in this unit are undated, continuing the narrative suspension between the first Babylonian deportation (597 BCE) and the final fall of Jerusalem (586 BCE). A notable exception appears in Ezekiel 20:1, which is carefully marked as "the seventh year, in the fifth month" (590 BCE) — approximately one year after the vision in Ezekiel 8–11. The setting, in which elders approach the prophet to inquire of YHWH, triggers one of the scroll's most theologically complex responses: a sweeping review of Israel's covenantal failures from Egypt to exile. This single timestamp re-anchors the section within the growing arc of judgment, even as surrounding oracles drift without temporal anchoring.

The literary time here stretches. No longer driven by dramatic vision or symbolic performance, these chapters adopt a slower rhetorical pace. They function almost like extended disputations, in which theological arguments are layered, reiterated, and sharpened. The narrator seems to seize the temporal ambiguity as a space of interpretive freedom — taking time to speak what must be spoken before history overtakes the audience.

This decelerated tempo does not lessen the urgency. Instead, it reframes it. These oracles should not be read as post-fall reflections. Rather, they unfold within the shadow of catastrophe—spoken while loss is still imminent, not after it has been realized. Their voices are sober, unhurried, but firm because they offer a kind of pre-traumatic witness. The prophetic task in this window is not to repair, but to name. Not to soothe, but to expose. Ezekiel 12–23 thus becomes a suspended corridor of theological confrontation: time slows, but pressure builds.

Communicative Flow

In Ezekiel 12–23, the communicative structure intensifies the asymmetry already introduced earlier: God speaks more urgently, Ezekiel performs more dramatically, and the audience retreats further into narrative absence.

Sender: YHWH speaks with growing rhetorical force and frustration. The tone becomes more severe, but the mode remains one-sided. Even when the oracles cite human speech, it is framed within divine quotation—appropriated for rebuke, not granted dialogical space.

Messenger: Ezekiel continues to mediate divine messages, primarily through embodied critique rather than direct proclamation. This unit includes one of the densest concentrations of reported prophetic performances, all in Ezekiel 12. The first enactment—described and explicitly performed (12:7)—portrays the general exile of the people. The second and third, revealed the following day, symbolically dramatize the desperate flight of King Zedekiah and his coming downfall. Though only the first act is narratively confirmed, all three carry distinct narrative purposes: to shock, to interpret, and to foretell. These non-verbal performances—especially when paired with eating acts (e.g., 12:18)—could demonstrate how the prophet's own body becomes a medium of judgment.

Receiver: The audience remains largely undefined. While oracles frequently address "the house of Israel," they seldom include real-time reactions. When the elders do appear (e.g., Ezekiel 14; 20), they are rhetorically overruled. Their questions are not answered; they are recast into charges. Rather than being allowed to speak, they are spoken about—folded into YHWH's accusatory frame.

Narrative Gaps: Enacted signs are described but rarely resolved within the narrative. Audience perception is presumed but not recorded. No communal transformation occurs. What remains is a scroll structured by divine initiative and prophetic performance—but one still suspended without confirmed reception.

Form and Genre

This unit exhibits some of the most diverse and complex literary forms in Ezekiel.

Symbolic Action: Chapter 12 dramatizes exile through Ezekiel's day-and-night bag-packing ritual.

Allegory: Chapters 16 and 23 present extended personifications of Jerusalem and Samaria as promiscuous sisters (Oholah and Oholibah).

Royal Parable with Interpretive Layering: Chapter 17 introduces a fable-like allegory of two eagles and a vine. On the surface, it reflects international politics—Babylon, Egypt, and Judah—but its interpretive conclusion reframes the narrative theologically, exposing Judah's violation of covenant and reinforcing divine sovereignty.

Theological Disputation: Chapter 18 stages a direct rebuttal of the proverb about generational guilt, asserting individual responsibility.

Lament: Chapter 19's dirge for the royal house, using animal metaphor, evokes dynastic collapse without invoking hope.

Historical Recitation and Covenant Parable: Chapter 20 offers a lengthy historical rehearsal that reinterprets Israel's past through a covenantal lens. The structure is triadic: in Egypt (20:5-9), in the wilderness (20:10-26), and in the land (20:27-29), each movement marked by divine grace and human rebellion. This rehearsal not only reframes the present exile as a continuation of wilderness judgment, but also anticipates restoration. However, the rhetorical failure of this mode is underscored in the closing verse (20:49), where Ezekiel laments that the people mock him as merely "one who speaks in parables." Even within divine persuasion, communicative breakdown persists.

Symbols and Keywords

Wall and Digging (Ezekiel 12:3-7): Ezekiel is instructed to perform an exile drama by packing his belongings and digging through a wall in plain sight. The "wall" symbolizes the fragile boundary between the illusion of security and the coming collapse. The act of digging through the wall prefigures the attempted nighttime escape of King Zedekiah during the final siege of Jerusalem (cf. 2 Kings 25:4-5; Jer. 39:4). He is the "prince in Jerusalem" referenced in Ezekiel 12:10, who will try to flee but be captured and blinded — fulfilling the oracle that he would be taken to Babylon but not see it (Ezek. 12:13).

Whitewashed Wall (Ezekiel 13:10-15): The metaphor of the whitewashed wall critiques the messages of false prophets — likely those in Jerusalem or among the exiles — who proclaim peace when destruction is imminent. The wall is painted to appear stable, but its structural flaws guarantee collapse. The image highlights theological deceit and denial of impending judgment.

Sisters Samaria and Jerusalem (Ezekiel 16 and 23): In a pair of graphic allegories, Samaria and Jerusalem are depicted as sisters named Oholah and Oholibah, representing the northern and southern kingdoms, respectively. Their sexual promiscuity symbolizes political alliances with foreign powers (Egypt, Assyria, Babylon) and covenant infidelity. These chapters do not merely moralize but offer a political- theological indictment of imperial idolatry, illustrating how betrayal is layered — national, spiritual, and intimate.

Eagle and Vine (ch. 17): A cryptic parable of political betrayal — Babylon and Egypt appear as empires offering false security.

Lioness and Cubs (Ezekiel 19:1–9): The lioness represents Judah as the royal house of David, and her cubs are captive Judean kings. The first cub is likely Jehoahaz (Shallum), who was taken to Egypt by Pharaoh Necho (cf. 2 Kings 23:31–34), and the second is Jehoiachin, exiled to Babylon after only three months on the throne (2 Kings 24:8–12). This lamentation reveals dynastic disintegration: young lions raised to rule are instead captured, caged, and silenced.

Thematic Functions

Chapters 12–23 deepen the theological and rhetorical intensity of Ezekiel's message, laying bare tensions that the earlier visions had only begun to articulate. If Ezekiel 4–7 built toward the visionary exposure of desecration in Ezekiel 8–11 — culminating in temple defilement, civic collapse, and divine departure — this unit sustains and intensifies that arc. These chapters stretch toward the stormfront of chapter 24, preparing both prophet and reader for the final breach of Jerusalem. In this sense, 12–23 functions as a theological tempest gathering force: not simply offering more judgment, but actively training the audience to receive it without nostalgia or misplaced sympathy.

Thematically, this section wrestles with unresolved contradictions and divine provocations. The discourse of responsibility versus inheritance reaches a climax in chapter 18, where the proverb of generational guilt is decisively overturned: "The soul who sins shall die." At the same time, mercy is deferred — divine judgment accelerates, but compassion is not offered as a rhetorical counterweight. This asymmetry intensifies the emotional and theological stakes of the scroll.

Divine frustration becomes increasingly audible, especially in chapter 20, where YHWH's historical rehearsal shifts not toward persuasion but toward justification of abandonment. The failed history of obedience is rehearsed not as prelude to repentance but as rationale for exile. Similarly, the disturbing theology of violence in chapters 16 and 23 — framed through metaphors of adultery, infanticide, and military brutality — risks theological scandal. Yet these tropes unmask the political and spiritual devastation caused by imperial entanglements.

Finally, exile is redefined as more than punishment: it becomes the collapse of covenantal imagination. With kings fallen, cities personified and ruined, and the divine voice unreciprocated, the text frames exile as theological exhaustion. These chapters invite the reader not into sympathy with Jerusalem, but into a reckoning with its desecration. They press the audience to ask not how to mourn the past, but how to survive its collapse.

In the Classroom

In this session, students will analyze Ezekiel 18

to discuss whether divine justice is based on individuals or the community as a whole. They will explore how divine justice relates to community responsibility, especially concerning collective guilt in society. As participants discuss, they will examine how this chapter revises their understanding of covenants and prompts them to consider themes such as responsibility, generational guilt, and moral choices.

Next, lead students through an ethical reading of the allegory, focusing particularly on chapters 16 and 23. Encourage students to unpack the layered metaphors within these texts and reflect on how such imagery both amplifies and complicates the prophetic critique. It will be essential to help students navigate the ethical tensions posed by gendered and violent symbolism— inviting them to ask not only what the text means, but how it communicates, and at what cost.

To deepen their interpretive skills, students will also engage with Ezekiel 17 through the lens of literary parody and theological satire. Pair this chapter with selected modern political cartoons to illustrate how metaphor and critique function together. Use this as a springboard for dialogue on the rhetorical power of satire in sacred texts—how humor can carry the weight of theological judgment without trivializing it.

Finally, guide students in the creation of a visual timeline linking major historical events—such as Zedekiah's reign, the successive deportations, and the fall of Jerusalem—with the oracles in chapters 12–23. This timeline should not only trace events but also visually demonstrate the entwinement of history and prophetic imagination. Encourage students to annotate their timelines with key themes, symbolic acts, and rhetorical shifts, helping them see how Ezekiel's message is inseparable from its moment.

Preaching Ezekiel 12–23 demands courage. These chapters do not offer redemptive closure. They call the congregation to confront theological exhaustion—where promises have become proverbs, and hope sounds like sarcasm.

In particular, Ezekiel 13's indictment of "peace where there is no peace" challenges the preachers to resist easy consolation. Chapter 18 allows for a sermon on moral agency—but with gravity, not flattery. The preacher must interpret not only divine judgment, but divine disappointment.

Above all, these chapters are a summons to integrity. The scroll does not ask, "Are you hopeful?" It asks, "Are you honest?"

Ezekiel 24: Boiling Judgment, Silent Collapse

Ezekiel 24 marks a critical threshold in the prophetic narrative: the moment when Jerusalem's doom, long foretold, becomes a historical fact. The chapter opens with an oracle dated to the very day the Babylonian siege of Jerusalem begins—"this very day" (24:2)—collapsing the distance between divine speech and historical catastrophe. What follows is the parable of the boiling pot (24:3–14), a symbol previously used in Ezekiel 11 but now intensified. Here, the pot no longer merely contains the city; it becomes the site of unrelenting purification. Bones are boiled, scum clings to the metal, and the fire is stoked until impurity is exposed and consumed. The metaphor refuses resolution. The pot is not emptied—it is scorched. Judgment does not cleanse; it burns.

Yet the symbolic heat of the first oracle gives way to the emotional desolation of the second. On that same day, Ezekiel's wife dies, and he is divinely prohibited from mourning her loss (24:15–27). This

71

personal rupture becomes a national allegory: just as the prophet must mute his grief, so too will the people be silenced before the fall of their beloved city. The prophet's body becomes the scroll's syntax; his silence, a grammar of judgment. This double oracle—boiling violence and suppressed lament—forms the theological and ethical epicenter of the entire scroll. In a world where covenant has collapsed and memory has failed, speech itself fractures. What cannot be mourned must be embodied. What cannot be spoken must be endured.

Literary Time

The date formula in Ezekiel 24:1—"in the ninth year, in the tenth month, on the tenth day of the month"—marks one of the most precise and momentous time-stamps in the book. This is the very day Jerusalem came under siege (cf. 2 Kings 25:1), transforming the prophet's role from foretelling to witnessing. It is a decisive narrative pivot: theological projection collides with historical trauma. What had been visionary, symbolic, or anticipatory now becomes real, named in synchrony with political catastrophe.

This is the only moment in the first half of the scroll where prophetic time and historical time fully converge. Up until this point, Ezekiel's messages have been spoken in advance of judgment, hovering in an atmosphere of suspended warning. Here, however, divine speech and imperial violence occur simultaneously. The rhetorical timeline tightens. The prophet no longer imagines the fall—he inhabits its first day.

Ezekiel 24 thus functions as a theological and literary hinge. It is the final date formula in the book's judgment arc, concluding a long series of oracles that spanned from Ezekiel 1 through 23. It seals the end of prophetic anticipation and opens the door to irreversible consequences. In literary time, it is both culmination and collapse.

Importantly, this chapter also reconfigures the prophet's body as a sign. The sudden death of Ezekiel's wife becomes the scroll's last symbolic action before the fall, rendering grief itself unutterable. Here, prophetic silence does not signify muteness alone — it becomes the only faithful expression of a world unraveling in real time.

This is no longer a space for rhetorical persuasion. It is not a moment for new warnings. It is the day the siege begins. Any attempt to read Ezekiel 24 as a post-fall reflection misreads its narrative placement and theological tension. The prophet speaks into catastrophe, not after it. The scroll's voice is not retrospective but concurrent — bearing witness in the very hour when speech ceases and judgment arrives.

Communicative Flow

Ezekiel 24 presents two oracles with sharply contrasting communicative dynamics. The first, the boiling pot allegory (24:3–14), follows the familiar Ezekielian pattern: the divine sender issues a command, whether or not the symbolic action is actually performed, the text does not confirm it — thus maintaining a rhetorical displacement in which the audience overhears a message not directly addressed to them. YHWH instructs Ezekiel to "utter a parable toward the rebellious house" (24:3), targeting those still in the Land. Though the action is described, its performance remains unconfirmed. Yet the message names an absent audience in the Land, displacing the exiles into the role of overhearers whose reflective engagement is invited but never overtly demanded. This second-person address ("you") is reserved for the virtual recipients — the inhabitants of Jerusalem. This rhetorical strategy, a hallmark of the scroll, uses unreachable targets to provoke theological reflection in those who can still hear. The absent are accused so the present may awaken.

By contrast, the second half of the chapter — the death of Ezekiel's wife and the prohibition to mourn (24:15–27) — displays an unusually full communicative triangle. Here, the Sender (YHWH) issues an immediate, non-negotiable command; the Messenger (Ezekiel) embodies the message through personal suffering; and the Receiver (the exilic community) responds verbally. This is one of the rare instances in Ezekiel where the audience's speech is explicitly narrated: "Will you not tell us what these things mean for us?" (24:19). The interaction is brief, but the fact of response marks a shift. Interpretation is not assumed; it is demanded.

This dual structure dramatizes the tension between distance and immediacy in prophetic communication. The boiling pot oracle burns with indirect judgment, casting the present audience as overhearers of a message for someone else. The wife's death oracle, in contrast, demands affective alignment: the exiles must mirror Ezekiel's silence, absorbing national catastrophe without ritual or lament. In this paradox, the scroll enacts its own tension between clarity and concealment. It withholds emotional resolution even as it offers theological clarity.

The narrative, finally, builds silence into its structure. While the audience speaks, no divine reply is given. The grief remains suspended — unspoken, embodied, and waiting for a future word.

Form and Genre

Ezekiel 24 presents a striking literary hybrid. It

opens with an allegorical parable—a boiling pot (24:3 14) that evokes and intensifies the earlier imagery of chapter 11, now as a scene of inescapable judgment and irreparable impurity. This is followed by a prophetic sign-act, as Ezekiel's wife dies and he is explicitly forbidden to mourn (24:15-18). The narrative then shifts into an oracular pronouncement, interpreting the prophet's private grief as a public sign: just as he must remain silent, so too the exiles will be too stunned by Jerusalem's fall to perform communal mourning rites. This genre layering heightens theological urgency through embodied silence.

Symbols and Keywords

Ezekiel 24 employs symbols that move from divine grief to prophetic embodiment and finally to communal paralysis. The boiling pot (24:3-13) returns from earlier imagery but now signifies irreversible judgment: Jerusalem, as a corroded vessel, cannot be cleansed by ordinary means. The rusted scum clings too deeply, and only through total incineration can impurity be exposed. This sets the stage for divine rupture.

The death of Ezekiel's wife (24:15-18), called "the delight of [his] eyes," mirrors the desecration of the temple—YHWH's own beloved dwelling. Yet Ezekiel is denied the right to mourn. His silence enacts the theological claim that when divine presence withdraws, even lament must cease. This prohibition extends to the people (24:21-24): their children and sanctuary will fall, but they must not cry.

This is not the silence of apathy but of restrained compassion. What unfolds is the final stage of divine self-withholding—the moment just before the tear might fall, the sigh might escape. The God of Ezekiel 24 is not unmoved; he is brimming with anguish, holding back consolation lest it interfere with judgment that must now come. The refusal to mourn, then, is not denial of feeling, but the performance of divine ache held in check. It is as though God says, "Hold it in, just a little longer—it's nearly complete." This is not cruelty but the last contour of mercy: pain deliberately postponed so that justice can be fully seen. To mourn too soon would lessen the weight of what must be faced. Hence, Ezekiel's silence mirrors God's own—an exhausted but deliberate pause before the next act of restoration.

Thematic Functions

Ezekiel 24 stands as the theological and narrative threshold of the entire scroll—a pivot where divine judgment reaches its saturation point and the long-prepared rupture becomes irreversible. The burning pot (vv. 3–14), the death of the prophet's wife (vv. 15–24), and the desecration of the temple (v. 21) collectively mark the incineration of what once held sacred meaning. These are not symbolic gestures from a distance; they are acts in which YHWH himself is deeply entangled. God commands, but God also grieves. The divine initiative pierces its own body— destroying the sanctuary, taking Ezekiel's wife, and offering no room for mourning—not because God is untouched, but because he is utterly invested. YHWH here emerges as a wounded reformer, willing to enact devastation upon what he once inhabited to clear space for something holy to begin anew.

This chapter renders prophetic speech ethically ambiguous. Is it compassionate to name grief when even grief must be withheld? Ezekiel becomes the vessel of divine restraint, feeling loss but forbidden to process it. His silenced body replaces the spoken oracle. The scroll itself mimics the logic of this grief—muted, distorted, suspended. There is no plea, no lament, no return offered here—only rupture, command, and the divine ache that underwrites them all. This is not yet re-creation, but it is its terrible threshold.

In the Classroom

Exegetical Lab: Compare the boiling pot in Ezekiel 24 with that in Jeremiah 1. How does each prophet deploy heat, metal, and impurity to frame divine action?

Trauma Pedagogy: Invite discussion on how theological texts handle communal trauma without language. What are the ethics of prophetic silence?

Embodied Reading: Assign a student to read Ezekiel's lines in 24:15–18 without emotion. What does it feel like to "perform" divine mourning without lament?

Preaching Insights

To preach Ezekiel 24 is to bear witness to silence. Not to explain suffering, but to mark it. The preacher here is not a voice of clarity, but a keeper of rupture.

The death of Ezekiel's wife—a personal horror turned national sign—forces the congregation to see grief that has no outlet. This is not a sermon for comfort. It is a liturgy of stunned witness, where hope must wait behind the curtain of divine absence.

The message is not that God is gone—but that even God sometimes withholds grief until the judgment is fully seen. Preachers do not resolve this tension. They guard it and name it holy.

Ezekiel 25–32: Foreign Nations as Israel's Mirror

Between Jerusalem's imminent downfall (chapter 24) and the revival of prophetic discourse directed at Israel (chapter 33), Ezekiel shifts his focus outward. Or does he? Chapters 25–32 present YHWH's oracles against various foreign nations—Ammon, Moab, Edom, Philistia, Tyre, Sidon, and Egypt—but their underlying purpose is more nuanced. These chapters act as a rhetorical mirror: God's judgments against "the others" serve to reframe the concept of divine justice for Israel. The narrative, previously centered on the corruption of Jerusalem, now utilizes the nations as a reflective foil, offering indirect commentary and theological insights.

Literary Time

These chapters span from 587 to 571 BCE—beginning after the siege of Jerusalem (Ezekiel 24:2) and mostly preceding the announcement of the city's fall in Ezekiel 33:21. While some oracles—such as that in Ezekiel 29:17—were delivered much later, the book places them within a suspended narrative window between judgment and restoration.

Unusually for the book, many of these oracles are precisely dated, creating a chronological surface that appears stable and linear. Yet their function in literary time is far more complex.

This section serves as a deliberate narrative suspension—a widening of the interpretive gap between the moment of catastrophe and the moment it is publicly confirmed. While the reader waits for news of Jerusalem's fate, the passage directs attention elsewhere: to the nations. The oracles against Ammon, Moab, Edom, Tyre, Egypt, and others do not merely displace attention; they reframe it. The narrator seems to slow the reader down, stretching narrative time to allow theological reorientation.

In this interval, the destruction of Jerusalem is not forgotten but refracted. From the vantage point of international judgment, Israel's fall is placed within a larger map of divine justice. YHWH's sovereignty is not confined to Zion—it expands across boundaries. In this way, the oracles against the nations offer more than polemic; they create an interpretive field in which the trauma of Jerusalem's fall can be read as part of a broader theological movement.

The scroll does not rush toward restoration. It holds the reader in this suspended time, inviting them to reconsider what judgment means—not as isolated punishment, but as part of a divine purging that implicates all nations. The prophet is silent about Jerusalem's outcome, but the silence is strategic. By the time the news of fall finally arrives in Ezekiel 33:21, the reader has been given space—not just to absorb judgment, but to reimagine its scope.

Communicative Flow

In Ezekiel 25–32, the prophet delivers a series of oracles ostensibly aimed at foreign nations—Ammon, Moab, Edom, Philistia, Tyre, Sidon, and Egypt. On the surface, these speeches appear to be diplomatic denunciations or geopolitical condemnations. Yet the communicative structure reveals something more subtle and inward-facing. The nations addressed are not present, nor is there any recorded response from them. Their rhetorical function is not participatory but illustrative. These oracles operate as rhetorically displaced speech-acts: they are voiced against distant others but crafted for the ethical and theological reflection of those nearby—the exiles in Babylon.

In this sense, the real audience is not the nations, but Israel. God speaks through Ezekiel "to" foreign kings, cities, and empires—but in a way that draws Israel into overhearing. The prophetic voice functions almost as theological ventriloquism: divine speech is

79

thrown outward, only to boomerang back as moral pedagogy. The nations become distorted mirrors, reflecting Israel's own fallen pride, idolatry, and misplaced confidence.

YHWH remains the sender, addressing the nations through Ezekiel's oracular imagination. The prophet himself does not travel abroad or deliver these messages in person; rather, he speaks about the nations to the exiles. Even this delivery is textually ambiguous — whether these speeches were actually uttered aloud in communal settings remains uncertain.

Thus, while the formal addressees of these oracles are foreign powers, the functional recipients are Israel's displaced people. The oracles destabilize assumptions of Israel's moral superiority by showing that other nations, too, are judged — not for covenantal infidelity, but for pride, violence, and exploitation. The message is not triumphalism, but alignment: God's justice is universal, and Israel's suffering is not unique.

In this communicative logic, the prophet becomes a staging agent, speaking "to others" to shepherd his own community toward theological recalibration. The exilic audience must learn to hear foreign judgment as self-implicating revelation.

Form and Genre

Ezekiel 25–32 deploys a diverse array of literary forms to pronounce judgment on foreign nations. Woe oracles express divine denunciation in the mode of lament, often directed toward specific cities such as Tyre (Ezekiel 27) and Egypt (Ezekiel 32). Mythic parody heightens the rhetorical force: the king of Tyre is cast as a fallen Edenic figure (28:11, 19), while Pharaoh is likened to a monstrous sea dragon (29:3; 32:2), evoking both hubris and chaos. Dirges and laments further intensify the message — chapter 27, for example, extols

Tyre's maritime elegance before narrating her symbolic shipwreck, while chapters 30–32 grieve Egypt's downfall through royal funeral motifs.

These genres are framed within broader prophetic judgment speeches, where each nation is named for its pride, violence, or betrayal against Israel. The literary artistry of these chapters renders foreign demise both mournful and instructive, inviting the exilic audience to discern divine justice not through triumphalism but through a stylized grief that reinforces covenantal reorientation.

Symbols and Keywords

Ezekiel's oracles against the nations are rich with mythic imagery and metaphor, transforming historical judgment into theological poetry. The following symbols illuminate how empires fall not only through politics, but through cosmic and moral disintegration.

Sea Monster (tannîn): Pharaoh is imagined as a crocodile or chaos-dragon in the Nile (29:3). This symbol links imperial Egypt with primordial disorder— recalling the cosmic battles of creation myths.

Shipwreck (Tyre): The great trading empire is likened to a beautiful ship shattered at sea (27:25–36). Her fall dramatizes the fragility of the global economy and human pride.

Staff of Reed (29:6–7): Egypt is depicted as an unreliable ally—its promised support breaks and wounds. This metaphor links prophetic critique with the erosion of geopolitical trust.

Pit (Sheol): Chapter 32 catalogs Egypt's descent into the underworld alongside other fallen nations—a chilling roll call of imperial hubris laid low.

Thematic Functions

Ezekiel 25–32 functions not only as a denunciation of foreign nations but also as a form of theological reorientation for Israel. At one level, these oracles affirm divine vindication: YHWH's justice is not parochial or tribal. Just as Jerusalem fell for covenantal betrayal, so too are Ammon, Moab, Edom, Tyre, Sidon, and Egypt judged for arrogance, opportunism, or exploitation. The principle is not ethnic, but ethical. This theological parity challenges any lingering assumption that Israel's suffering is unique or undeserved. More subtly, these oracles operate as indirect mirrors: the grandeur of Tyre and Egypt—described in lyrical and even admiring tones—is ultimately dismantled. In this way, Ezekiel critiques not only the nations but also Israel's own illusions of exceptionalism, cautioning the exiles against misplaced nostalgia or imperial envy.

Through their fall, YHWH re-centers the narrative: the true sovereign of history is not Babylon, nor Pharaoh, but YHWH alone. Political powers rise and fall, but divine sovereignty remains constant. These oracles thus become pedagogical, training Israel to recognize judgment not as randomness, but as covenantal logic applied across all nations—including their own.

In the Classroom

Mapping Empires: Have students trace each oracle's geographical and historical context. How does space function rhetorically?

Myth in Prophecy: Analyze the Edenic and Leviathan motifs. How do these symbols reshape national histories?

Literary Lament: Assign different students to read dirges from chapters 27, 30, and 32 aloud. Discuss the role of stylized grief in judgment.

Preaching Insights

To preach from Ezekiel 25–32 is to risk misdirection—and that's the point. These chapters appear to target "the others," but they're really aimed inward. They teach that critique is safest when distant— but most needed when near.

The preacher must resist using these texts to reinforce nationalist triumphalism or moral superiority. Instead, they are tools of humility. The rise and fall of nations are not just a historical lesson—it is a theological one. Judgment is not a show of power; it is a mirror demanding a response.

Ezekiel 33–34: The Collapse of Silence and the Descent of the Shepherd

Ezekiel 33–34 represents a pivotal threshold in the theological and literary architecture of the book. The long-delayed news of Jerusalem's fall finally arrives—not as a surprise, but as confirmation of prophetic warning, marking the collapse of enforced silence and the reanimation of divine speech. Yet the moment is anything but celebratory. Rather than vindication through repentance, Ezekiel encounters a community that listens but does not respond, admires but does not obey. In this liminal space between catastrophe and restoration, the prophetic voice is reframed: no longer a herald of judgment, Ezekiel becomes a witness of ruin and a conduit for unexpected compassion. What follows is one of the book's most radical theological shifts— YHWH's decision to shepherd the people directly. Together, these chapters offer not just a literary hinge, but a theological turning, where divine presence reenters history not through structures, but through intimacy.

Literary Time

This section opens with a pivotal timestamp: "In the twelfth year of our exile, in the tenth month, on the fifth day…" (Ezekiel 33:21). A fugitive arrives from Jerusalem, bringing the long-anticipated news: the city has fallen. Although the destruction had occurred over a year earlier (586 BCE), this delayed report—narratively placed in 585 BCE—marks far more than a historical update. It signals the end of prophetic suspense and the start of a new theological phase.

The next verse announces a profound shift: "My mouth was opened, and I was no longer mute" (33:22). This moment ends the silence imposed in Ezekiel 24 and inaugurates a different kind of prophetic role. Ezekiel is no longer a watchman warning of coming disaster; he becomes a witness to the aftermath, commissioned to speak into a space already emptied by judgment. The urgency that once leaned forward now leans downward—toward accountability, restoration, and pastoral redefinition.

Yet the recommissioning does not rush into comfort. What follows in Ezekiel 33–34 is not triumphal hope but sobering confrontation. God speaks again—not to pronounce new judgments, but to reclaim responsibility for the scattered flock. The shepherd oracles of Ezekiel 34 mark a crucial transition: divine speech now gathers rather than scatters. Still tethered to the memory of devastation, this section initiates a shift from prophetic exposure to redemptive reconfiguration.

In literary time, Ezekiel 33–34 forms the hinge between catastrophic silence and constructive renewal. It opens the post-siege space with neither immediate consolation nor rhetorical relief, but with the slow, deliberate work of restoration through responsibility. This is not yet restoration proper, but it is the clearing of ground—an opening made possible only after collapse has been named and endured.

Timeline: From Deportation to Fall (597–586 BCE)

Year (BCE)	Ezekiel's Reference	Event	Literary Placement
597 BCE	Beginning of exile (cf. Ezek 1:2)	First Babylonian deportation (Jehoiachin exiled)	Ezekiel's prophetic call context
592 BCE	5th year of exile (1:2)	Ezekiel's inaugural vision by the Chebar canal	Ezekiel 1–3
591 BCE	6th year (8:1)	Vision of the Jerusalem Temple	Ezekiel 8–11
590 BC	7th year (20:1)	Elders inquire; historical review of rebellion	Ezekiel 20
588 BCE	9th year, 10th month, 10th day (24:1–2)	The second Babylonian siege begins	Ezekiel 24
586 BCE	11th year (cf. 2 Kings 25:2–4)	Jerusalem Fell (temple destroyed)	The event occurs; it has not yet been reported.
~585 BCE	12th year, 10th month, 5th day (33:21)	Fugitive arrives in Babylon with news of the fall	Ezekiel 33:21–22: turning point of speech

Communicative Flow

Ezekiel 33–34 stages a complete shift in prophetic communication: In Chapter 33, Ezekiel is reappointed as a watchman—not to warn of what is coming, but to interpret what has already happened. The people's stunned reaction ("How can we live?" 33:10) reveals an existential crisis. Yet their final response is troubling: "They hear your words but do not do them… to them, you are like one who sings love songs with a beautiful voice." (33:32)

The prophet becomes background music. His fulfillment is aestheticized, not heeded. In Chapter 34, the divine voice overtakes all human intermediaries. Shepherds—kings, priests, prophets—are indicted as predators.

"I myself will search for my sheep." (34:11) In this radical realignment, God refuses to delegate. Communication becomes direct, compassionate, and sovereign. YHWH does not appoint new leaders—He replaces them. Where human leadership failed, divine presence descends. Regarding the communication flow, readers would likely recognize this significant change, but whether the immediate audience understands it remains uncertain.

Form and Genre

Ezekiel 33–34 forms a pivotal literary and theological hinge within the scroll, combining diverse genres to mark the transition from judgment to restoration. Ezekiel 33 opens with a legal-theological metaphor: the prophet is cast again as a *watchman* (vv. 1–9), responsible not for outcomes but for faithful warning. This metaphor is followed by an ethical disputation (vv. 10–20), where divine justice is defended against communal accusations of unfairness—a rare moment where theological reasoning is staged directly. The chapter then delivers its narrative climax (vv. 21–22), as the fugitive from Jerusalem arrives and Ezekiel's long-enforced muteness ends. The section closes with a prophetic satire (vv. 30–33), where the exilic audience is accused of treating Ezekiel's messages as entertainment, exposing the thin line between fascination and disregard.

Chapter 34 pivots dramatically into a covenant lawsuit (*rîb*) against Israel's leaders, recasting the kings as failed shepherds who consume rather than protect

(vv. 1–10). In response, YHWH issues a royal-pastoral oracle (vv. 11–31), declaring that He himself will seek, rescue, and tend the scattered sheep. Drawing from Ancient Near Eastern royal ideology, where kings are often titled "shepherds," Ezekiel subverts the trope: YHWH does not rule from a throne but descends into the field — embodying divine kingship as intimate care rather than distant sovereignty.

Symbols and Keywords

The symbolic vocabulary of Ezekiel 33–34 crystallizes the theological turn from collapse to divine reclamation, marking a shift in register from judgment to restorative intimacy.

Watchman (צָפָה / ṣāpāh): Initially a figure of foresight (cf. Ezekiel 3:17), the watchman is now reintroduced as a witness to the aftermath (Ezekiel 33:1–9). The symbolic burden has changed — from warning of the future to interpreting the consequences. This subtle shift echoes the prophet's own transition from silenced warning to post-catastrophe articulation.

Shepherds: Human leaders are portrayed as negligent and predatory. They feed themselves but not the flock, exposing a distortion of political and spiritual vocation. Their corrupt silence contrasts sharply with YHWH's self-declared voice: "I myself will search for my sheep" (34:11). The failed shepherds' abdication becomes the backdrop for divine intervention.

Flock / Scattered Sheep: The people are described as vulnerable, exiled, and unprotected, symbolizing more than physical dispersion. They are spiritually orphaned, caught between abandoned leadership and divine retrieval.

Cloud and Thick Darkness (עָנָן וַעֲרָפֶל / ʿānān wa-ʿărāpēl): These terms once conveyed divine inaccessibility, as in Exodus 20:21, where Moses

87

approaches God in obscurity. But in Ezekiel 34:12, this same imagery is reversed: YHWH pierces through the cloud and thick darkness "on a day of clouds," to retrieve the scattered. This reversal implies that YHWH has long remained hidden — voluntarily restrained in grief and judgment — until the moment comes for divine pursuit. This descent is not casual. It evokes a theology of self-imposed containment, wherein God breaks through layers of divine restraint, making this act of rescue a moment of profound intimacy. It approaches the theological register of incarnation — not in form, but in emotional and ethical cost.

Lovely Song (שִׁיר עֲגָב / *šîr ʿeḡeḇ*): In Ezekiel 33:32, the prophet's words are received not as a summons to repentance, but as performance. The people enjoy his voice "as one who sings love songs," but they do not act. This image indicts religious aestheticism: where truth is admired but not obeyed, and where the prophet becomes spectacle rather than moral provocateur.

Thematic Functions

Ezekiel 33–34 marks a decisive pivot in the scroll's theological movement. Before the turning point, we are given a final rationale for judgment (33:1–20) and an unexpected encouragement: that repentance is still met with divine readiness. These oracles do not simply justify the past — they seek to dignify the listener's moral agency even after catastrophe.

Then, in verses 21–22, the turning point arrives: a fugitive from Jerusalem reports its fall, and Ezekiel's mouth is opened. This moment marks more than a narrative shift — it constitutes a second prophetic commissioning. No longer bound to silence, Ezekiel moves from forecasting to interpreting. The exilic reality no longer needs to be predicted. It must now be understood.

Strikingly, this recommissioning does not yield immediate obedience. The people remain rebellious, described in 33:31–32 as listeners who enjoy Ezekiel's voice but ignore his words. Despite this, God does not respond with renewed judgment. Instead, divine initiative deepens in another direction.

Chapter 34 begins not with the people, but with their leaders. The oracle of indictment targets the shepherds of Israel—figures who have failed to protect, feed, or heal. But unlike earlier accusations, this one is immediately followed by replacement. God will become the shepherd. This signals a theological reconfiguration: divine agency will no longer work through broken intermediaries. It will act directly.

At the same time, the people, too, are transformed—not by their effort, but by divine promise. They will be gathered, restored, and given "a new heart" (cf. 36:26). As the chapter ends, what is secured is not territorial restoration or political reconstruction—but relational reconciliation. The shepherd finds the sheep. He binds wounds, brings the scattered to rest, and promises them peace.

Thus, the thematic function of Ezekiel 33–34 is to mark the scroll's movement from silence to speech, from exile to initiative, from collapse to covenantal renewal. Not by reversing time, but by reentering the relationship.

In the Classroom

Dialogical Role Play: Divide students into groups: failed shepherds, scattered sheep, and the divine Shepherd. Let each group reflect on their own theologies of abandonment, failure, and hope. Ask what it means to be found when you stop asking to be rescued?

Textual Contrast Exercise: Compare Ezekiel 33:32 ("lovely song") with Ezekiel 34:11–16 ("I myself will search…"). What does each reveal about the nature and risk of divine communication?

Theological Timeline Mapping: Have students build a timeline connecting the fall of Jerusalem, Ezekiel's recommissioning, and the descent of the Shepherd. Mark when silence reigned, and when it was broken — not only in time, but in tone.

Ethical Reflection Prompt: "If God leads like Ezekiel 34, what kind of leadership do we owe each other?" Encourage students to consider spiritual leadership in exile — when institutions collapse, and speech must begin again.

Preaching Insights

To preach Ezekiel 33–34 is to speak from the wreckage — not as triumph, but as holy interruption. The prophet is not vindicated by response, but by the truth he bore in silence. And when God speaks again, it is not to reassign roles — but to arrive in person.

"I will rescue them from all the places where they were scattered on a day of clouds and thick darkness." (34:12) Here, the preacher is challenged to proclaim not the repentance of the people, but the unrelenting movement of the Shepherd: The flock does not call. The Shepherd moves first. The darkness is not lifted — it is entered. What kind of God seeks the lost before they realize they are missing? What kind of preacher dares to speak when no one listens, and yet cannot stop because God has spoken again?

Ezekiel 35–36: Two Mountains, One Future — Judgment, Silence, and the Geography of Restoration

In Ezekiel 35–36, the book turns from individual judgment to spatial transformation. Rather than addressing people directly, God now speaks to landscapes. Two mountains—Mount Seir and the Mountains of Israel—are cast as opposing theological agents: one condemned, the other called to blossom. These chapters prepare the soil—both literally and theologically—for the return of the resurrected dry bones in chapter 37. In this transition, Ezekiel emphasizes divine initiative over human repentance and focuses on re-creation through sanctified geography rather than a return to Jerusalem.

Literary Time

No precise date formulas appear in this section. Still, its placement is strategic: it follows the reported fall of Jerusalem (Ezekiel 33–34) and immediately precedes the visionary restoration of the people in Ezekiel 37. The narrative thus floats in a state of post-catastrophic suspension, emphasizing theological sequence rather than chronological detail. What emerges here is not a moment in time, but a spatial and symbolic reordering.

This sequence echoes the pattern of Genesis 1–2: space must be ordered before life can inhabit it. The land must be addressed before the people return. In Ezekiel 36, the mountains of Israel are personified as witnesses to judgment, desecration, and future renewal. The absence of human dialogue is striking—YHWH speaks to the land, not through the people. Restoration begins without human initiative, suggesting that the land itself holds covenantal memory and bears the trauma of abandonment.

The preceding oracle against Mount Seir (Ezekiel 35) reinforces this spatial-theological logic: Edom's opportunistic violence is condemned precisely because it violated the sacred timing of divine judgment. In contrast, Israel's mountains are prepared for renewal—not because of their people's righteousness, but for the sake of YHWH's name. Time is suspended here not because nothing is happening, but because something foundational is being laid beneath the surface: a terrain capable of holding grace.

In literary time, Ezekiel 35–36 offers a theological reset. It delays the restoration of Israel's people by attending first to the condition of their land — its desecration, its silence, and its potential. What seems passive is deeply preparatory. Only after the land has been addressed, healed, and re-spoken into covenantal alignment will the bones be gathered and breath return.

Communicative Flow

In Ezekiel 35–36, the communicative structure shifts strikingly: YHWH does not address people directly but rather speaks to the terrain itself. The prophet Ezekiel functions not as a persuader of human hearers but as a mediating presence — standing between divine speech and an unresponsive audience. The recipients of these oracles are not individuals or nations but symbolic landscapes: Mount Seir (representing Edom) and the Mountains of Israel.

This rhetorical strategy operates through proleptic displacement. Although the language targets landforms, the real audience is the exilic community, who are implicitly invited to overhear. In the absence of direct human response, the terrain becomes a surrogate listener — a canvas onto which divine judgment and hope are projected. Through this shift, the land assumes dual roles: as both sermon and sanctuary, absorbing the emotional intensity of God's words and reflecting the spiritual condition of the people.

By speaking to the mountains, YHWH paradoxically speaks to those who dwell far from them. The exilic audience is thus reoriented — not by being addressed, but by witnessing God's voice reclaim and repurpose the very ground that had once rejected them. In this moment of theological silence, the land becomes eloquent.

Form and Genre

Ezekiel 35–36 employs a striking literary juxtaposition: the oracles against Mount Seir (Edom) in chapter 35 form a covenant lawsuit (*rîb*), while chapter 36 transitions into lyrical prophecy filled with restoration motifs. The genres are deliberately staged: Ezekiel 35 is an accusatory address of ancestral hostility, echoing texts like Obadiah and Psalm 137, where Edom's betrayal during Jerusalem's fall is recast as theological enmity. The indictment is framed not only against Edom's violence, but against its gloating—the sin of assuming possession over land that belongs to YHWH.

Ezekiel 36, by contrast, is a poetic cascade of generative speech. It moves from scorn to soil, from barrenness to fruitfulness, from shame to re-creation. The prophetic voice shifts from litigating enemy violence to promising internal renewal. The land itself becomes both audience and agent: "But you, mountains of Israel..." (36:8). This personification of landscape creates a prophetic ecology, where geography is no longer a neutral background but an active partner in covenantal repair.

Together, the two chapters dramatize a theological reversal: one mountain is silenced for overreaching, while the other is revived to receive exiles. The genre movement—from *rîb* to re-creation— traces divine intent not only to judge injustice, but to cultivate possibility.

Symbols and Keywords

Ezekiel 35–36 reconfigures Israel's geographic

and relational imagination by assigning moral significance to mountains and names. These symbolic elements encode historical trauma, divine intent, and eschatological hope within the land itself.

Mount Seir (Edom): Kin turned enemy. Seir becomes a symbol of gloating kinship, opportunistic violence, and anti-covenantal mockery. Edom's desire to possess the land of Israel is presented not as mere geopolitical ambition, but as theological trespass—a violation of sacred inheritance.

Mountains of Israel: Edenic terrain made desolate now called to "shoot forth branches" (36:8), reversing the land's exile. The mountains are no longer backdrops to human failure but active participants in divine renewal. Their rejuvenation anticipates the return not just of people, but of covenant order.

Final Mention of "Jerusalem" (36:38): The name "Jerusalem" disappears after this chapter, signaling a deliberate narrative shift—from corrupted memory to transformed identity. When the city is named again in Ezekiel 48:35, it is not as "Jerusalem" but as "YHWH *Shammah*" —"The LORD is There." Geography itself becomes liturgical.

Thematic Functions

Ezekiel 35–36 enacts a theological inversion: from judgment to creation, from people-centered responsibility to land-centered promise, and from human repentance to divine initiative. These chapters are not merely transitional—they recalibrate the entire moral architecture of restoration.

God does not wait for Israel to repent. Instead, God acts "for the sake of [his] holy name" (36:22). This re-centers covenantal renewal not on merit but on divine fidelity. Restoration becomes an act of holy self-consistency. The land becomes responsive, obedient—

"hearing" the word of God in contrast to the people who have persistently failed to listen. Where human conscience has become deafened, the soil itself becomes the first site of response.

Mount Seir's judgment in chapter 35 functions as an ethical prelude: justice must be served before healing can begin. But in chapter 36, the mountains of Israel are addressed as living entities, called to "shoot forth branches" and welcome their people home. The regenerative work begins not in human hearts, but in terrain, topography, and tilled ground.

This return-from-the-ground anticipates the resurrection logic of Ezekiel 37. Just as in Genesis 1, where the land, light, and boundaries are prepared before humanity is formed, Ezekiel's vision replays a kind of theological cosplay of creation. The bones will rise — but only after the earth is made holy again.

In the Classroom

Geopolitical Intertextuality: Compare Edom's downfall in Ezekiel 35 with Obadiah and Psalm 137. How is kinship weaponized in prophetic critique?

Theological Geography: Why does God speak to mountains? Explore prophetic displacement and spatial imagination.

Jerusalem's Erasure: Have students trace the final mention of "Jerusalem" and consider its replacement in Ezekiel 48. What does renaming signal theologically?

Optional Classroom Visual: Create a comparative chart of Mount Seir and the Mountains of Israel, showing contrasts in audience, tone, outcome, and symbolic function.

Preaching Insights

Preach Ezekiel 36 as a re-creation theology.

95

Before reviving people, God tills the soil. Restoration begins where no one is watching—with land, with silence, with seeds.

Let the sermon ask: What if God is already healing the ground beneath our unawareness? What if grace begins before we repent? What if we are latecomers to a garden already growing?

This chapter is not a call to action, but an invitation to witness divine gardening—where God's covenant faithfulness blossoms in soil still stained by grief.

Ezekiel 37: Breath, Bones, and the Blueprint of Re-Creation

Ezekiel 37 stands as one of the most iconic and theologically dense moments in the book—not because restoration is fulfilled, but because it is uttered into possibility. Set in a valley of utter desolation, this chapter does not open with a date but with a question: "Can these bones live?" (37:3). In the wake of divine silence, failed leadership, and fractured land (chs. 33–36), this vision unfolds as a post-collapse intervention, where language itself must be reassembled alongside the bones. The prophet is not given an audience, only a task—to speak to death, to summon breath, and to perform hope before it is visible. What emerges is not resurrection as comfort, but re-creation as divine initiative: an act of Spirit that moves before understanding, and a covenant that binds what history has severed.

Literary Time

Ezekiel 37 emerges not in the middle of disaster, but after it. It follows the announced collapse of Jerusalem (Ezekiel 33), the redefinition of leadership through the shepherd oracle (Ezekiel 34), and the theological reclamation of space in the twin mountain oracles (Ezekiel 35–36). Yet no new date formula appears. The vision unfolds in an untimed interval—a theological "after" that resists anchoring in history. This is not restoration in progress; it is resurrection imagined.

The literary time here is shaped by silence. The nation is not yet revived, but the ground has been cleared. The valley of dry bones holds no signs of agency or petition. The prophet is not sent to warn or judge, but to witness—to stand in the middle of death's totality and wait for divine breath. The absence of time-markers deepens the sense of stillness: this is a moment unmeasured by clocks, but weighted with expectancy.

Ezekiel is commanded to prophesy not to people, but to bones; not to rebels, but to remnants. Speech precedes response; breath precedes recognition. The narrative reverses the earlier logic of cause and effect—here, life precedes repentance, and restoration comes not as a reward but as a miracle. The prophet's task is not to interpret, but to obey—to speak into what cannot respond.

In literary time, Ezekiel 37 stands as a theological hinge between collapse and covenant. It is the moment when divine imagination interrupts historical inevitability. While no specific date is given in the text, the vision unfolds in a theological moment beyond history—a divine initiative that marks the beginning of resurrection, not its aftermath.

Communicative Flow

Both visions—of dry bones and the two sticks— are explicitly staged by YHWH and mediated entirely through Ezekiel. The audience, again, is not the original historical group but the future reader or hearer. This fits within the rhetorical displacement strategy already evident throughout Ezekiel: unreachable or absent targets (e.g., Jerusalem, deceased ancestors, scattered tribes) are addressed to mirror those present (the exilic community). The communication is vertical (between YHWH and Ezekiel) and performative rather than dialogical.

These paired visions of revivification and reunification thus function as a divine soliloquy performed for a misaligned audience. The dry bones prophecy is directed to "the whole house of Israel" (37:11), which, though already dead and dispersed, is still addressed in the present tense — as if the word alone could undo death.

The prophet becomes a mediator not between God and people, but between silence and Spirit. He speaks not to listeners, but to matter — to bones and winds. This defamiliarizes communication itself. What does prophecy look like when the only audience is death?

Form and Genre

Ezekiel 37 is one of the most theologically and literarily layered chapters in the Book of Ezekiel, fusing visionary drama, symbolic action, and covenantal proclamation into a unified movement of resurrection and reunification. It functions as a performative hinge: theologically expansive and rhetorically immersive.

The first section (vv. 1–14) unfolds as a visionary performance. The prophet is led by the hand of YHWH into a valley of dry bones — a visual tableau of total desolation. What follows is a liturgical sequence of commands and responses: "Prophesy over these bones," "Say to the breath," "Come from the four winds." These speech acts are not descriptive but generative, transforming inert fragments into embodied life. The scene evokes a ritual theater where language performs resurrection.

The second section (vv. 15–28) shifts to a symbolic action: Ezekiel is told to take two sticks — marked for Judah and Joseph — and join them into one. This prophetic gesture, accompanied by divine interpretation, announces the reunification of the divided kingdoms under a renewed covenant. The narrative form combines enacted symbolism with oracular clarity.

Intertextually, the entire chapter is saturated with creation motifs, particularly from Genesis 2. The Hebrew *ruach* (spirit/wind/breath) mirrors the divine breath that animated Adam, signaling that this is not just political restoration, but ontological re-creation.

Thus, Ezekiel 37 transcends a single genre. It is a prophetic enactment, a theological performance, and a cosmic echo. It moves from metaphor (dry bones) to history (return) to promise (unified covenant) — each stage layering vision upon symbol, and symbol upon speech.

Symbols and Keywords

Ezekiel 37 offers some of the most potent symbolic imagery in the prophetic canon — imagery that bridges desolation and restoration, fracture and reunion, silence and breath. The symbolism is deliberately layered, requiring both imaginative immersion and theological patience.

Dry Bones (37:1–2): The valley is not merely filled with the dead — it is filled with bones long disassembled, "very dry," stripped of flesh, sinew, and memory. This is a vision of total loss: not only death, but the erasure of form, identity, and coherence. The image functions intertextually as a reversal of Genesis 2 and evokes apocalyptic visions of battlefield ruin. Yet the divine question, "Son of man, can these bones

99

live?" (37:3), is met not with logic but with surrender: "O Lord YHWH, you know." This moment of epistemic humility recalls Peter's response to Jesus in John 21:17 — "Lord, you know all things; you know that I love you" — uttered in a similarly restorative moment after betrayal and loss. In both texts, hope is rekindled not through certainty, but through relational trust in divine knowledge.

Breath / Spirit (רוּחַ, *ruah*): This Hebrew term carries a deliberate triple meaning: wind, breath, and Spirit. Ezekiel's vision exploits this polyvalence to suggest that what revives Israel is not merely air or spirit in the abstract, but the uncontainable movement of divine will. Ruach enters the bones not at the prophet's discretion, but only through God's initiative — reinforcing that resurrection is never mechanized, but always relational and bestowed.

Two Sticks (37:15-28): The symbolic act of joining the sticks labeled for Judah and Ephraim marks the transition from resurrection to reunification. What begins as bodily reanimation culminates in national cohesion. While David is explicitly named in Ezekiel 37:24-25, the reference does not reinstate a dynastic ruler from Judah. Rather, "David" serves as a symbolic shepherd embodying the restoration of the eternal covenant. The focus thus shifts from royal conquest to pastoral care and covenantal fidelity.

Together, these symbols trace a movement from scattered bones to rejoined sticks — from private ruin to public reconciliation. The vision gives form to the unfathomable: that God's breath can reanimate what history has discarded, and that a people fragmented by exile can be made one again under a renewed covenant and an unambiguous shepherd.

Thematic Functions

Ezekiel 37 renders restoration not as consolation but as divine commissioning. The vision of dry bones encompasses more than a single historical calamity. Temporally, it stretches back to the deaths in Egypt and the wilderness — where bones were left unburied as signs of rebellion — and forward to the current exilic trauma. Spatially, it gestures not just to the land of Israel, but to all the places where people have died, been dispersed, deported, or forgotten. The deliberate abstraction of the valley's location and timeframe creates an open scope that makes the resurrection vision paradigmatic rather than localized.

This is not resurrection for the sake of comfort — it is restoration as a mandate. Bones come together, but without breath, they remain corpses. The prophet must prophesy again, this time to the *ruach* (Spirit/breath/wind), making clear that restoration without divine Spirit is only animated death. Hope without holiness is a hollow frame.

Moreover, the absence of human repentance is striking. This revival is not earned by moral reformation but enacted by divine initiative. The staff symbolism in the second half (vv. 15–28) points to political reunification, but without royal nostalgia. Instead of an empire, a "covenant of peace" (v. 26) is offered. And the temple — now deferred — is a future presence, not a current achievement. Restoration, then, is not a return to old forms, but a reconstitution in alignment with divine purpose.

In the Classroom

Breath Exercise: Assign students to explore "ruach" across Ezekiel 1, 2, 3, and 37. How does meaning shift?

Exilic Theater: Perform the vision with two readers (YHWH and Ezekiel), with students as the bones. Explore timing and hesitation in the prophetic response.

Political Reflection: Debate the difference between reunion (sticks) and resurrection (bones). What does Ezekiel say about divided communities?

Preaching Insights

Ezekiel 37 is not a sentimental tale of resurrection—it is a prophetic rehearsal for reconstitution in the wake of irreparable loss. Preachers must resist the urge to romanticize its imagery. The bones are not simply tired—they are disassembled. There is no sinew, no breath, no hope. And yet, they are told to listen. Not because they can respond, but because God wills them to live.

This is not revival born of repentance, but restoration initiated by divine speech. Just as YHWH once withdrew from the temple (Ezekiel 10–11), now the breath returns—not to stone, but to the broken community. Re-creation precedes readiness. God's Spirit enters before the people even know what it means to be whole.

In John 21, a similarly broken Peter, asked whether he loves Jesus, can only say, "Lord, you know." It is a confession from someone beyond certainty, beyond repair—yet still summoned. The preacher might echo that moment here: when faced with dry bones—of faith, community, or future-the only true reply may be: "Sovereign Lord, you alone know" (Ezek 37:3).

To preach this chapter is to invite listeners not to feel strong before believing, but to trust that divine breath comes not after strength, but before it.

Ezekiel 38–39: Purging the Land: Gog, Judgment, and Liturgical Thresholds

Ezekiel 38–39 stages a final, unrelenting confrontation not with a historical empire, but with the theological residue of chaos. Positioned after the vision of dry bones and national reunification (ch. 37) but before the detailed vision of the new temple (chs. 40–48), these chapters inhabit a liminal zone between resurrection and habitation. Gog of Magog — summoned, not simply permitted — embodies opposition that must be ritually extinguished before divine presence can return to dwell. Here, eschatology becomes liturgy: divine warfare is less a battle than a purification, and Israel's role is not to fight, but to cleanse, bury, and remember. This is not geopolitical fantasy but sacred threshold drama, where bones are no longer merely revived, but named and interred. The land must not only be restored — it must be made holy.

Literary Time

Ezekiel 38–39 contains no specific date formula, but its placement within the scroll is highly intentional. The vision arrives after the resurrection of dry bones (Ezekiel 37), where national restoration is declared, but before the revelation of divine indwelling in the temple vision of Ezekiel 40–48. Israel is described as "dwelling securely" (38:11) — not in naïve presumption, but in a divinely granted state of stability. The land has been restored, the people reconstituted, and no judgment oracle is directed at them.

Yet into this sanctified calm enters an unexpected threat: Gog from the land of Magog. His arrival, however, is not autonomous. YHWH explicitly draws him in — placing hooks in his jaws (38:4), stirring his movement (38:16), and orchestrating the encounter.

103

Israel does not provoke the war that unfolds, nor is it permitted by chance. It is divinely staged, not to discipline Israel, but to expose and eradicate what does not belong.

In literary time, this battle functions not as the climax of restoration, but as a final purification before God's glory would return to the newly built temple (Ezekiel 43). The land has been made clean; Israel now functions like a priestly body, silently occupying sacred space. Gog's intrusion constitutes a breach between the profane and the holy. YHWH alone responds—not as a military commander, but as the sovereign guardian of sanctity.

The silence of Israel is therefore not passivity but posture. The people are not called to fight because they have already been set apart. Their presence affirms divine order; their inaction signals priestly separation. Gog does not threaten them directly—he threatens the boundary of holiness that God has now reestablished.

The lack of a date intensifies the symbolic charge of this moment. The scene unfolds in a suspended liturgical frame, between spatial restoration and divine indwelling. Before the new temple can be revealed, the land must be purged. What appears to be an external battle is, in fact, a priestly defense of sacred order. It is YHWH—not Israel—who enforces the final act of separation, making way for the return of glory in Ezekiel 40–48.

Communicative Flow

Ezekiel 38–39 stages a cosmic confrontation, but its communicative dynamics are not aimed solely at the enemy. Instead, the vision performs a rhetorical drama in which Israel is the true overhearer. The Sender is YHWH, who not only predicts but actively summons Gog—an adversary drawn by divine hook, not personal ambition (38:4). The Messenger is Ezekiel, who delivers both the call to battle and the interpretation of its aftermath. The named Addressee is Gog (38:2), yet the actual audience is Israel, who overhears the charges and must reckon with their implications.

This indirect address follows a recurring Ezekielian strategy: prophetic speech to displaced entities—mountains (6:2), gates (11:1), bones (37:4)—which mirrors back theological insight to Israel. Here, addressing Gog serves as an eschatological mirror: the final judgment is not merely about defeating enemies, but about purifying the land to make space for YHWH's return. Israel is not the target, but the inheritor of the vision's consequences.

Form and Genre

Ezekiel 38–39 combines elements of: Apocalyptic vision – cosmic battle and divine intervention; Covenant lawsuit – a trial against Gog, resulting in destruction; Liturgical lamentation – the scavenger feast and burial rites; and Priestly purification – bone-marking, weapon-burning, land-cleansing

Each form intensifies the sense of finality and ritual closure. The grotesque details—corpse burial, seven-year fire, carrion feast—transform warfare into sacrificial drama, echoing Leviticus and Deuteronomy's logic of *herem* (total destruction for divine sanctification).

Symbols and Keywords

Ezekiel 38–39 is thick with symbolic reversals and ritualized language. Though stylized as an apocalyptic battle, the episode is more liturgical than military. Its imagery reconfigures destruction into purification, inviting the audience to reinterpret victory through priestly and spatial categories rather than imperial triumph. Each symbol thus becomes not only a narrative device, but a theological signal for transition and threshold.

Gog of Magog: A mythic enemy representing ultimate opposition to YHWH's reign. Gog is not a historical figure but a theological foil—summoned by YHWH only to be destroyed, underscoring divine initiative (38:4).

Weapons Burning (39:9–10): Israel uses Gog's weapons as fuel for seven years—both a symbolic cleansing and a reversal of dependence. What once threatened life now sustains it.

Mass Burial (39:11–16): The valley of Hamon-Gog becomes a necropolis. Israel performs a priestly role by cleansing the land through burial, naming bones, and erecting markers.

Birds' Feast (39:17–20): The feast for scavengers mimics sacrificial rites (cf. Rev. 19) but reverses them—enemies are not worshippers, but offerings. This grotesque liturgy emphasizes divine dominance.

Hamon-Gog: "The multitude of Gog" becomes both a burial site and a memory site, solidifying the transition from desecrated land to a re-consecrated one.

Together, these images render Gog's defeat not as an epic war tale, but as a ritual of purification. The vision does not glorify violence but repurposes it. Israel's task is not to fight, but to remember, bury, and sanctify. Restoration comes not through conquest, but through ritual transformation—a fitting threshold to the temple vision that follows.

In the Classroom

Ritual Mapping: Chart the sequence from resurrection (ch. 37) to purification (chs. 38–39) to sanctuary (chs. 40–48). How is holiness architected?

Role Enactment: Assign Gog, Ezekiel, and the bone buriers. Reflect on each role's theological burden.

Textual Juxtaposition: Compare Leviticus 26, Revelation 19, and Ezekiel 39. What convergences and tensions emerge in their handling of judgment and sanctity?

Key Prompt: Why is Gog necessary after the bones rise? What does it mean that God purifies the land before entering it?

Preaching Insights

Preach Ezekiel 38–39 not as a prediction of end-time warfare, but as a dramatized threshold. Gog is not future terror; he is final impurity. His erasure marks the opening for YHWH's return.

The preacher's task is not to explain Gog's identity, but to reveal God's liturgical logic: no resurrection without purification. No presence without sanctified space.

Gog's downfall is not a national victory — it is a priestly burden. The sermon becomes a call to carry that burden: to mark the bones, bury the past, and tend the land until holiness can return. "What would it mean," the preacher might ask, "if the holiest thing we could do is bury what God destroyed — so that His presence might come again?"

Ezekiel 40–48: The Temple Vision and the Architecture of Preventive Holiness

Ezekiel's final vision suspends resolution in favor of revelation. Unlike previous oracles that appeal to emotion or exhortation, this temple-centered sequence unfolds with austere precision: measurements, boundaries, altars, gates. There is no high priest, no ark, no singing crowd—only a prophet who sees, walks, and records. Restoration here is not framed as nostalgic return but as architectural restraint: a design of sacred space structured to prevent relapse. The absence of political actors, the subordination of the *nāśî*, and the meticulous zoning of holy and profane mark a shift from emotional repentance to spatial discipline. The temple does not descend into history nor arise from communal effort; it floats—evocative of Ezekiel 1's mobile throne—as a visionary construct inviting internalization. The vision hovers above, accessible not by construction but by contemplation. In this sense, Ezekiel 40–48 closes not with arrival, but with orientation: a mapped holiness that does not celebrate restoration but safeguards it.

Literary Time

The timestamp in Ezekiel 40:1—"In the twenty-fifth year of our exile, at the beginning of the year, on the tenth day of the month"—stands out for both its precision and its interpretive openness. This formula differs from other date formulas in Ezekiel. It uniquely contains the phrase *Rosh Hashanah* (beginning of the year), thereby underscoring its exceptional theological and narrative status. While the Book of Ezekiel contains multiple date formulas, none is as liturgically evocative as this one. A comparison with Ezekiel 29:17 clarifies the stakes: though it also uses a similar structure, that oracle simply reads, "on the first day of the first (month)," without explicitly using the phrase *Rosh Hashanah*. The difference suggests that, unlike 29:17, Ezekiel 40:1 opens a liturgical prism of meanings. The ambiguity lies in the fact that two major Jewish calendar systems—civil and cultic—offer competing interpretations of when "the beginning of the year" falls.

If one reads Ezekiel 40:1 through the lens of the civil calendar, *Rosh Hashanah* refers to the first day of Tishri, and the "tenth day" would then point to *Yom Kippur*. If one opts for the cultic calendar rooted in Exodus 12:2, then "the beginning of the year" signals Nisan as the first month, and the tenth day would instead point to Passover preparation, specifically the day the lamb is selected (Exod 12:3).

What makes this ambiguity productive rather than problematic is its narrative and theological placement. It's important to note that the dual interpretive possibilities arise not from textual uncertainty but from the compositional approach to the vision. If one assumes the vision was directly received and accurately conveyed by Ezekiel, then he would have had a specific date in mind, either Nisan or Tishri.

Conversely, if one views the vision as a literary construct by an implied author, the mention of *Rosh Hashanah* might suggest an intentional ambiguity within the text itself.

Reading 1: Tishri 10 – Yom Kippur as the Framework

If the reference is to the tenth day of Tishri, then Ezekiel receives this temple vision on *Yom Kippur*, the Day of Atonement. This reading aligns with the prophetic context: the temple had been destroyed; the people had been defiled. Now, on the very day that marked national repentance and sanctuary cleansing (Lev 16), Ezekiel is shown a new sanctuary. The theological resonance is strong: before the glory returns, the space must be redefined.

Furthermore, *Yom Kippur* is followed by *Sukkot* (Tishri 15–21), the feast that commemorates Israel's wilderness dwellings after the Exodus. Notably, *Sukkot* is not celebrated in the wilderness itself, but only after

Israel enters the land. Thus, the *Yom Kippur* framework suggests that this vision occurs in the final days of wandering, preparing for renewed, permanent dwelling. The sequence of *Yom Kippur* to *Sukkot* becomes a symbolic arc: purification → re-dwelling → joy.

In the wider liturgical tradition, the ten days between *Rosh Hashanah* (Tishri 1) and *Yom Kippur* form the *Yamim Nora'im*, the Days of Awe—a time for reflection, repentance, and preparation for divine encounter. Ezekiel's vision thus stands at the climax of this sacred tension, offering a visual answer to a season of silence and judgment.

Reading 2: Nisan 10 – Passover Preparation and Prophetic Urgency

Alternatively, reading Ezekiel 40:1 as Nisan 10 places the vision within Passover preparation. In Exodus 12:3, God instructs Israel to select a lamb on the tenth day of Nisan and to keep it until the fourteenth, when it will be sacrificed. That liminal period— dwelling with the lamb marked for death—was to prepare the people for the night of distinction and escape.

In this frame, Ezekiel's exilic community becomes analogous to Israel in Egypt: living under threat, yet preparing for divine deliverance. Ezekiel sees the temple not as a site of arrival, but as a promise held in tension—a lamb dwelling with the people, awaiting redemption. The temple is chosen, measured, and revealed, but not yet filled with glory. Its presence signifies a coming exodus.

Further interpretive depth arises when we compare Ezekiel 40 with Joshua 4:19, where the Israelites cross the Jordan and enter the Promised Land precisely on Nisan 10. At that first entry, the subsequent Passover was marked by the sobering reality that only two individuals from the Exodus generation had survived to see it. By contrast, the anticipated second entry from Babylonia — if Ezekiel 40 is read as occurring on Nisan 10 — is marked by synchronicity, publicity, and tribal unity. No tribe is excluded; no remnant is left wandering. The vision signals a new kind of entry: one in which no generation is doomed to die in the wilderness. Rather than being fragmented by death and delay, the community crosses over together, fully gathered and fully seen.

This interpretation is further strengthened by the vision of dry bones in Ezekiel 37:1–11, which explicitly identifies the resurrected figures as "the whole house of Israel," extending the scope of return and restoration both temporally and geographically. Moreover, the subsequent oracles depict a reunification of the tribes of Judah and Joseph, signaling a post-Babylonian future in which such profound national reconciliation becomes possible. The return is unified, measured, and sanctified.

Theological Convergence: Not Either/Or, But Deepened Both/And

Rather than selecting one reading over the other, Ezekiel 40:1 seems to be deliberately situated to evoke both. The dual plausibility of *Yom Kippur* and Nisan 10 strengthens the theological force of the temple vision: it is both atonement and anticipation, both reentry and exodus, both purification and distinction.

Communicative Flow

In Ezekiel 40–48, the communicative dynamic undergoes a profound transformation. Unlike Moses or David, Ezekiel is not commanded to build a sanctuary or lead a community into liturgical renewal. Instead, he is instructed to observe, to measure, and to record: "Tell the house of Israel everything you see" (40:4; cf. 43:10). His role is not that of an active leader but a visionary scribe—tasked with documenting a temple that exists only in divine imagination.

The entire encounter is structured as a visionary tour. Ezekiel is guided through a fully formed architectural reality, but no implementation is commanded, and no human figures appear within that space. There are no worshippers, no high priests, no rituals performed—only walls, gates, measurements, and divine presence. Restoration here is not enacted but revealed.

Significantly, the audience is not Ezekiel's contemporaries but a deferred people—those who, having undergone judgment and exile, may one day experience shame and become receptive to holiness (43:10-11). The temple vision thus becomes a narrated sanctuary, a conceptual and theological space meant to be carried inwardly, rather than physically reconstructed.

The communicative structure reflects this distance. YHWH speaks only through the contours of sacred space; Ezekiel transmits, not preaches. The intended recipients are unnamed, absent, and perhaps even unborn. The silence is not incidental—it is architectural. There are no exhortations, no immediate reactions. Restoration is neither immediate nor dialogical; it is embedded in vision and awaits inhabitation by a healed imagination.

Form and Genre

Chapters 40–48 read as a hybrid of apocalyptic vision and priestly instruction: 40–42: Detailed architectural measurements; 43–46: Cultic regulations and sacrificial systems; and 47–48: Cosmic reordering of land and tribal boundaries.

This structure parallels Exodus 25–31 and later Revelation 21–22, yet with key differences: There is no builder, no altar liturgy, no communal inauguration. Measurements are often incomplete (e.g., no temple height), reinforcing its nature as a conceptual schema, not a construction blueprint.

The land allocations (ch. 47–48) remove contested territories (e.g., Transjordan) and relocate tribes symmetrically — utopian but not heavenly. This is not heaven. This is a survivable ideal, anchored not in transcendence but in concrete regulation. As Soo Kim Sweeney puts it, too fantastical for realism, too structured for eschaton. It is a mental scroll, sustaining the exiled with structured possibility.

Symbols and Keywords

This vision contains radical discontinuities: The walls are thicker (40:5), creating hardened boundaries between sacred and profane. Behind the Holy of Holies is a mysterious chamber (41:12–15) — YHWH's private space, never entered. No space is allocated for Transjordan, subtly erasing regions of previous rebellion.

Yet, continuities remain: Zadokite priests return, highlighting cultic lineage (44:15–31). A Davidic prince appears — not as king, but as a subordinate figure (45:7–17). Twelve tribes and Levitical laws are re-inscribed, linking the vision to Mosaic roots. The city is no longer called Jerusalem but YHWH *Shammah* (48:35) — "YHWH is there." This renaming is cosmetic; it marks a complete theological reorientation. The city becomes a pointer, a gatekeeper, a liturgical compass — not a monarchic capital or cultic center.

Symbolic Geography of Ezekiel 38–48: Three Peaks, Two Layers

The Temple (North, Highest Peak)

Symbolic Function: This is the restored sacred center. It represents the reentry of divine presence (Ezekiel 43), not through nostalgic memory, but through a newly measured holiness.

Location: To the north of the symbolic city YHWH *Shammah*, elevated and set apart.

Role: Acts as a holy beacon, visible yet restricted, a theological source of holiness. It corresponds with Levitical blueprints but exceeds them in abstraction.

YHWH Shammah (Center, Middle Elevation)

Symbolic Function: The new city replacing old Jerusalem, renamed "YHWH is there" (48:35).

Layering: This city overlays the memory of Jerusalem. It is not identical, but situated at the same site, thus suggesting a resurrection of identity through renaming.

Role: A gatekeeper city, linking sacred space (Temple) and purged space (Hamon-Gog). It performs a mediating function, neither sanctuary nor battlefield, but a pointer toward the holy.

Hamon-Gog (South, Lowest Peak)

Symbolic Function: The valley of final purification, associated with the burial of Gog's army (Ezekiel 39).

Geographic Logic: Likely in the southeastern region, near the Dead Sea, echoing the traditional placement of the Valley of Achor—a space of shame and purification.

Role: This is Death's Gate, the location of final judgment and ritual cleansing. It seals off the past and secures the land for divine indwelling.

Lower Layer: Jerusalem (Old)
Not erased but buried within memory. It is the spiritual substratum upon which YHWH *Shammah* is built. Like Palimpsest cities, the new overlays the old, honoring its existence while superseding its failed structures.

Upper Layer: YHWH Shammah
The new identity, replacing the name but preserving sacred geography. The city connects upward to the Temple and downward to the burial valley, forming a vertical axis of transition from shame to sanctification.

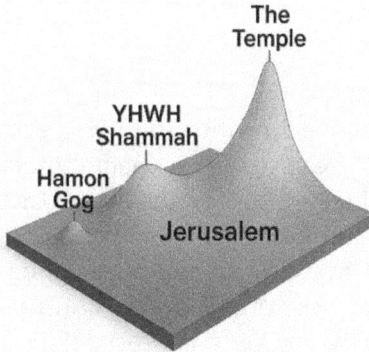

This 3D illustration models the theological geography of the final chapters of Ezekiel as a layered, tripartite landscape — not just in terms of physical elevation, but in symbolic meaning and narrative role.

Theological Message
Not Eschatological Heaven: This temple and city are not heavenly Jerusalem. There are still bones,

burials, corrections, and shame management. This is not the final consummation, but the beginning of disciplined restoration.

Architectural Memory: The landscape is curated for moral remembrance. Restoration is not indulgent— it is structured and monitored.

Double Gatekeeping: Hamon-Gog guards the southern gate, blocking shame and the return of impurity. YHWH *Shammah* guards the northern gate, pointing forward to divine re-entry and inviting vigilance.

Interpretive Implication

This geography invites readers and exiles not to return to Jerusalem as it was—but to approach what it could become, through memory, structure, and sanctified vigilance. It is not a city of comfort, but a city of discipline, thresholds, and hope deferred yet preserved.

Thematic Functions

Ezekiel's restoration is not permissive—it is preventative. These chapters enact a theology of post-traumatic holiness. The city has been lost. The exile has redefined presence. What emerges now is not a nostalgic return, but architectural memory. Divine presence re-enters only when boundaries are re-drawn. Priestly access is restricted. Worship is ritualized. The community remains unnamed. Holiness here is safeguarded through distance.

In the Classroom

Ezekiel 40–48 presents an ideal opportunity for integrative, interdisciplinary learning. Its detailed vision combines architectural precision, theological imagination, and liturgical implication—making it a rich site for student engagement across biblical studies, ethics, and design. Rather than focusing solely on textual analysis, instructors can guide students into participatory interpretation, where space, silence, and absence become interpretive tools.

Spatial Ethics Project: Invite students to design their own "sacred space" with specific enforced limitations. What must be excluded to preserve the sanctity of what is within? How do gates, barriers, and gradations of access construct ethical meaning?

Liturgical Blueprint Workshop: Have students compare Ezekiel's visionary temple with the tabernacle of Exodus and Solomon's temple in 1 Kings 6–8. What are the theological and political assumptions behind each structure? What is revealed — and what is restrained?

Hermeneutics of Absence: Facilitate a seminar discussion on what is not in Ezekiel's final vision. Why is there no high priest, no ark, no visible communal worship? How might absence function not as loss but as theological redirection?

This vision invites students not only to read the temple, but to think through what holiness requires of space, structure, and silence.

Preaching Insights

Ezekiel 40–48 is not a commission to build, but a meditation on how to carry holiness through exile. The prophet is not an architect, but a witness to a structure so sacred it cannot be touched.

This vision was not intended to be built — at least, not yet. It was given to sustain, to create "a small sanctuary" in exile (11:16), one that lives in the imagination, not the landscape.

Preachers must resist eschatological over-reading. This is not Revelation 21 — it is the precondition for sacred return, the blueprint that helps a shattered people believe there might still be form, meaning, and presence.

The message at the end of Ezekiel doesn't land — it lifts. It waits, hovering above the text, like the glory above the temple. Not an ending — but an opening.

Ezekiel 40–48 is not easy to preach. But it offers one of Scripture's most profound theological turnings: hope without possession. The temple is drawn but not entered. God is there — but not everywhere. The preacher must name this architecture of restraint as part of divine mercy. What if restoration requires redesign? What if presence requires limitation? The call is not to reclaim, but to receive — with reverence and distance.

Conclusion to Part II

Ezekiel's architecture is not ornamental—it is theological. From symbol to silence, from vision to void, the book speaks through structure as much as through speech. In Part II, we've traced how the Book of Ezekiel unfolds its theology not through clarity, but through construction. Judgment is choreographed. Hope is gated. Speech is measured.

Chapters 4–5 moved from macrostructure to micro-performance—from the scroll's global design to its most jarring symbolic acts. Each passage signaled a rupture—whether through the silence of Ezekiel 24 or the architectural vision of chapters 40–48. Form, in Ezekiel, does not decorate content. It is content. This is not prophecy as persuasion—it is prophecy as infrastructure.

Part II has shown us that in Ezekiel, the shape of the scroll is the message: its disorientation, its delay, its sealed hope. The scroll is designed to open slowly. The people may be gone. The temple may be cold. But the vision persists.

What remains now is to ask: How do we live with this kind of scroll? That is the work of Part III.

Part III
Living with Ezekiel

Ezekiel is not a book one simply finishes; rather, it is a scroll that opens into disorientation and closes with a glance of hope. While Part II delves into rhetorical strategies and literary sequences, Part III shifts its focus toward theological reflections. This section does not primarily ask, "What and how did Ezekiel say?" but rather, "What must we now carry?" The reader transforms from an interpreter into a theological inheritor, bearing a scroll that remains vibrant with unresolved tension.

How does one coexist with a prophet whose body embodies divine rupture? What does it mean to preach from a text in which judgment silences speech, and restoration occurs without consent? Here, it is proposed that Ezekiel provides not a path back to what was lost, but a blueprint to prevent a return to the circumstances that led to the people's downfall. The prophet's vision is not one of nostalgia; it is architectural — designing boundaries where trauma once existed unconfined and mapping holiness where desecration had prevailed. Ezekiel is not merely a prophet of exile; he serves as a dramatist of prevention. Rather than attempting to resolve Ezekiel's contradictions, Part III embraces them. It identifies the gaps, charts the questions, and listens for the ethical reverberations of a God who both abandons and returns.

The chapters in Part III follow that trajectory through several lenses. Chapter 6 offers a thematic synthesis of Ezekiel's theological vocabularies, tracing

121

presence, judgment, and restoration across the scroll. Chapter 7 explores unresolved theological tensions that continue to shape its interpretive horizon. Chapter 8 reflects on Ezekiel's embodied prophecy and the ethics of trauma, reading the scroll through the lens of bodily experience and deferred communication. Chapter 9 considers the homiletic challenges and possibilities of preaching Ezekiel today. Chapter 10 concludes with a reading of Ezekiel's architecture of prevention, memory, and theological vigilance — inviting readers to walk with a scroll that remains open.

Chapter 6
Issues and Themes in the Book of Ezekiel

The book of Ezekiel presents a constellation of theological motifs — fierce, strange, and ultimately, unresolved. Rather than unfolding in systematic order, its theology is woven into vision, enactment, and silence. This chapter identifies five thematic axes that define the scroll's theological terrain.

Divine Presence and Absence? Or Divine Endurance?

Ezekiel's inaugural vision begins with a visual and spatial rupture: the *kavod* (glory) of YHWH appearing above the Chebar canal in Babylon, not in Jerusalem. The mobility of divine presence, shown through a chariot-throne borne by living creatures and intersecting wheels, destabilizes the theological expectation that holiness resides only within the temple or the holy land. From the very beginning, God's presence is shown to be dynamic, capable of movement — toward and away, both visible and hidden.

This mobility eventually gives way to what appears to be an absence: in Ezekiel 10–11, the *kavod* leaves the temple, first pausing at the threshold, then ascending from the city. The movement is not abrupt but staged, as though reluctant. Such a pattern has sometimes been read as an expression of divine rejection.

However, the internal cadence of the scroll suggests something more sustained: a theology of endurance. The slow departure reflects an unspoken endurance — a divine patience under pressure. This restraint is voiced most poignantly in Ezekiel 6:9: "I was broken by their whoring heart." In this moment, divine

123

anger and grief converge. The pathos is not theatrical but inward. Divine endurance emerges not as mere forbearance but as mutual suffering—an ache that continues even as the relationship collapses.

Moreover, the divine presence is not utterly gone. The holiness that once filled the temple is not extinguished but held in tension, accompanying the exiles in silence and loss. In this way, divine presence in Ezekiel is reframed as presence under constraint—compassionately withheld in order to allow for the possibility of re-creation. Ezekiel 11:16 reveals that YHWH has become for the exiles a *miqdash me'at*—a small sanctuary. While the main temple is abandoned to judgment, God offers a fragment of His presence in exile. This subtle theological gesture affirms that divine endurance is not only cosmic but communal: God remains among the people in diminished form. The exilic community is thus not entirely forsaken; they are drawn into a shared endurance.

Later, in Ezekiel 43, the glory returns—but not as a mere reversal. The re-entry is quiet, measured, and framed by precise boundaries. Ezekiel is not told to build this temple, only to observe and record. The new structure is marked not by exuberance but by caution. Its silence, symmetry, and spatial ordering serve as architectural echoes of divine restraint. This vision does not undo the exile—it reorients it, offering a sacred space carried in memory before it is realized in stone.

In this light, divine presence and absence in Ezekiel are not binary categories, but stages within a larger theological arc. YHWH departs not as rejection but to preserve holiness. He remains, in exile, as a *miqdash me'at*, enduring alongside the people. And when He returns, it is not with immediate consolation, but with careful design—inviting the people to match divine endurance with their own.

124

Thus, the prophetic witness in Ezekiel is of shared waiting. Divine endurance does not negate absence—it gives it shape, meaning, and eventually, direction.

Judgment and Justice

The first half of the scroll is dominated by oracles of judgment—metaphors of siege, blood, infidelity, and impurity. The prophet declares guilt with the voice of certainty. And yet, the violence of divine response remains ethically destabilizing. Can justice look like this? Ezekiel insists that YHWH's judgment is purgative rather than vindictive—meant to purge, not simply to punish. But this claim is not offered gently. The text does not dilute its trauma, nor does it invite easy theological justification. It asks the reader to hold the justice of God in one hand and the horror of exile in the other, without dropping either.

Embodied Prophecy

Unlike other prophets, Ezekiel's message is not only spoken—it is lived, gestured, and suffered. He is struck mute, bound, commanded to lie motionless for months, and eat defiled food. His wife dies, and he is forbidden to practice any mourning rituals. The prophet becomes the message. This raises questions of prophetic agency: Did he consent? Did he understand? What does it mean when God's word breaks not only stones, but the prophet's body? Ezekiel's embodiment pushes prophecy beyond proclamation and into performance— where theological truth is communicated through gesture, constraint, and even pain.

Communal Responsibility and Moral Reconfiguration

One of Ezekiel's most theologically consequential interventions is the reconfiguration of communal and generational responsibility. In a bold departure from the ancestral punishment formula found in the Decalogue—"visiting the iniquity of the fathers upon the children to the third and fourth generation" (Exod. 20:5)—Ezekiel 18 insists, "The soul who sins shall die." This oracle does not negate communal responsibility, nor does it advocate modern individualism. Rather, it distinguishes between inherited guilt and covenantal accountability. The prophet challenges the exilic generation not to blame their ancestors but to engage in collective repentance. While the community may still suffer consequences for the sins of its members—reflecting the enduring reality of moral entanglement—the theological emphasis has shifted: every generation, and indeed each person, is summoned to respond to YHWH with integrity.

Ezekiel's vision thus upholds a model of responsibility that is both personal and corporate. It rejects passive victimhood while affirming that sin has ripple effects within the covenant community. The call is not to isolation, but to a shared turning—a reconstitution of communal identity through mutual acknowledgment of wrongdoing and collective participation in renewal.

Yet the text also recognizes a painful moral asymmetry: when the community at large is corrupt, righteous individuals may lack the power to redirect the collective course. Such persons—innocent but implicated—often become isolated voices of protest, lamenting against the overwhelming tide. Ezekiel names them not only ethically but liturgically. In Ezekiel 9, this faithful minority is identified as "those who sigh and groan over all the abominations committed in Jerusalem" (v. 4). These mourners, far from being ignored, are divinely marked with a *tav* on their foreheads—a sign of preservation that echoes the Passover blood on Israelite doorposts (Exod. 12:7). They are spared not because they have withdrawn from the community, but because they have remained morally engaged within it.

This vision resonates with Jesus' later teaching, "Blessed are those who mourn, for they shall be comforted" (Matt. 5:4). Ezekiel 9 affirms that lament is not a failure of faith, but its fullest expression in a collapsing world. Through the groaning witness of the few, a remnant ethic emerges: even when the majority is unresponsive, divine attention rests on those who mourn in solidarity. They are not merely survivors — they are the seedbed of a new community.

Sacred Space and Re-territorialization

Though Ezekiel mourns the temple's desecration, he does not imagine its restoration as a simple return to former boundaries. Rather, the final movements of the book — including the burial of Gog's forces in Hamon-Gog (39:11 16) — recast land, people, and sacred identity through a logic of re-territorialization. What emerges is geography and a community transformed through enacted purification and covenantal renewal.

Hamon-Gog — literally "the multitude of Gog" — becomes a necropolis, a liminal site where the residue of cosmic opposition is buried by the people of Israel themselves. Here, the act of burial is neither incidental nor pragmatic; it is liturgical. The people transition from passive survivors to active priestly crews of the land, reclaiming territory not through conquest but through sacred labor. By marking bones and cleansing the land, they ritually prepare it for the return of YHWH's presence.

This re-territorialization extends beyond geography to vocation. Israel, having once been the object of judgment, now becomes its agent — not in violence, but in sanctification. The act of burial signals a theological inversion: those once counted among the dead (cf. ch. 37) are now the ones who minister to the dead. In performing this priestly duty, the people recover the vocation first spoken in Exodus 19 — to be a kingdom of priests and a holy nation mediating between YHWH and the nations.

The reconfiguration of sacred space in chapters 40–48 adheres to a particular logic: Priestly lines are redrawn, and the roles of the Levites and Zadokites are restructured for renewed service. Land is redistributed, with the allocations of tribes reorganized and sacred and secular zones clearly delineated anew. Jerusalem is given a new name; once merely a city that housed the Temple, it is now known as YHWH-*Shammah* — "The LORD is there" (48:35) — serving as a guide for pilgrims coming to experience the presence of God.

Thus, sacred space is not recovered from memory but constructed from the aftermath. The burial of Hamon-Gog is not an epilogue to conflict but an overture to presence. The people's movement from judged to priestly, from scattered to sanctifying, reframes their role: no longer a passive recipient of divine rescue, but an active mediator of divine holiness. In Ezekiel's vision, re-territorialization is a priestly task, and the land's readiness for glory depends not on military triumph but on the faithfulness of those who now prepare it.

Conclusion

The Book of Ezekiel demands theological vigilance and moral honesty. The themes identified in this chapter — presence, justice, embodiment, responsibility, and sacred space — do not resolve the book's tensions but deepen them. The following chapters will now ask: What happens when those tensions are not just interpreted, but lived? What becomes of a prophet whose suffering was scripted?

And how might communities today carry a scroll that refuses to close?

Chapter 7
The Prophet's Body, the Community's Trauma
Embodied Mediation in Ezekiel

Ezekiel does not simply speak for God — he is made to become the message. His body is conscripted into a divine theater, becoming both a symbol and a site of theological rupture. This chapter explores the prophet's body as a mediating surface — through which divine grief, judgment, and even regret are made visible. The trauma of the community is not merely spoken to but enacted within Ezekiel's very flesh. And in this performance, the scroll conveys pain without offering a promise of immediate healing.

The Prophet as Embodied Threshold

Ezekiel's prophetic identity is not given through speech but through transformation. He is silenced (Ezek 3:26), immobilized (4:4-8), contaminated (4:12-15), shaved (5:1-4), and bereaved (24:15-24). His body becomes the site of divine messages that words alone cannot convey.

This embodiment unsettles prophetic categories. He is not simply a mouthpiece but a threshold — where divine judgment, human suffering, and symbolic performance meet. The scroll repeatedly withholds interpretation, leaving the community — and the reader — to confront the implications without resolution.

Embodied Grief, Deferred Mourning, and Restoring the Forgotten: Ezekiel 24

The death of Ezekiel's wife — "the delight of your eyes" — marks the culmination of embodied prophecy (Ezek 24:15-27). He is forbidden to practice public mourning, a command that fractures both cultural norms and personal grief. The event is doubly symbolic: it reflects Jerusalem's imminent fall and God's own loss. Yet the text offers no comfort. There is no recorded response from the audience. The silence is deafening. What does it mean when grief is not shared, when mourning is not permitted? Ezekiel becomes a theological question rather than a pastoral answer.

But what if these prophetic performances are not simply illustrative? What if they are incarnational — not only reflecting divine pain but mediating it, visualizing YHWH's own internal devastation in the body of the prophet? In this frame, Ezekiel is not being distanced from God to suffer in his place, but is being *invited into* the divine experience: "Let them see with human eyes how I suffer." That is, Ezekiel's silent grief becomes a living icon of the God who restrains His compassion in order to purify His people. Holiness cannot be restored without costly rupture, and the prophet bears the weight of that rupture, not symbolically but corporeally.

If so, then the unspoken charge to readers and preachers today is not only to interpret the death of the prophet's wife as a sign-event, but to recover her *dignity*. She was not publicly mourned, not ritually buried, not remembered by name — yet her loss marked a divine threshold. In honoring her now, readers enact a delayed mourning that was forbidden in the moment. This is not merely literary recovery; it is theological repair. Preachers must challenge their communities to become, in retrospect, the mourners she was denied. In so doing, they not only dignify the prophetic wound but recognize the God who grieves in silence — and whose love, though veiled, endures through fire.

Ezekiel: *Homo Sacer*? Or a Companion to the Divine Pathos?

If we accept the interpretive logic outlined above, then Ezekiel 24 offers us a rare window into prophetic literature: divine vulnerability. The loss Ezekiel suffers is not merely his own — it echoes God's pain over the defilement and destruction of the covenantal relationship. The unspoken grief in Ezekiel 24 reflects a divine sorrow too deep for language. What if God is not only a judge, but also a griever? What if the divine command not to mourn is not a denial of pain, but an inscription of it? Ezekiel's obedience thus becomes not only faithful but complicit in divine suffering — a burden that reshapes prophetic vocation as sacrificial participation.

In this light, we may ask: Is Ezekiel a *homo sacer* — a figure marked by sacred exception and legal exclusion, as Giorgio Agamben theorizes — or is he a companion to divine pathos? The answer may be both. Indeed, Ezekiel displays many features of the *homo sacer*: he is stripped of ordinary legal or relational protections, denied public grief, and subject to commands that isolate him from the communal rhythms of mourning and consolation. He is sacred yet expendable, central yet excluded.

But this reading, while apt, is not sufficient. What emerges more strikingly in Ezekiel's case is a reversal within the structure of exceptionality itself. In Agamben's paradigm, the sovereign and the *homo sacer* define opposite ends of the legal spectrum — the sovereign suspends the law from above, while the *homo sacer* is excluded from the law from below. Yet in Ezekiel, we witness something unimaginable in

133

ancient Near Eastern theology: the sovereign God voluntarily takes on the position of the *homo sacer*. This act is not imposed—it is self-chosen. YHWH, having no choice but to be broken due to the long-standing covenantal relationship (6:9), chooses to remain in exile (11:16), chooses to endure desecration and delay, all for the sake of a necessary purification that will allow for re-creation.

This divine self-lowering is not abstract. It is enfleshed in Ezekiel's embodied acts. If we understand Ezekiel's gestures not merely as prophetic performance but as visible icons of divine pain, then the prophet is not merely a servant but a co-sufferer. God does not simply command suffering; He undergoes it. And Ezekiel becomes the mirror in which this divine endurance is refracted for the people.

The point of all this? Purification. Without cleansing, there can be no new creation. And for that cleansing to be legitimate, it must be accompanied by the deepest possible compassion—a compassion so profound that it must, for a time, be restrained. Ezekiel is thus called not only to proclaim judgment but to bear it. In this, he models for the exilic audience what it means to join God not in sovereignty but in suffering.

And yet, once this sacrificial moment has passed—once Jerusalem has fallen, and the grief is complete—what then? Here the text issues a silent homiletic invitation: to remember and to mourn. The one who was denied mourning—Ezekiel's wife—must not be forgotten. Her death, like so many others, became a symbol swallowed in silence. It is now the task of readers, hearers, and preachers to restore her honor. In doing so, they do not only remember a woman or a prophet—they participate in the divine pathos that dignifies even the most unspeakable losses.

Trauma, Archive, and Transmission: Prophecy as Shared Vulnerability

The Book of Ezekiel is not simply a prophetic document—it is a trauma archive. Its disjointed temporality, its silences and sudden ruptures, and its ambiguous audience responses all signal a text written and transmitted within a condition of fracture. The scroll does not narrate resolution; it suspends it.

A Traumatized Author

Ezekiel, as a prophetic figure, does not deliver divine speech with clarity or command. His role is marked by involuntary silences (e.g., 3:26; 24:27), by symbolic actions that isolate rather than persuade (chs. 4–5), and by the unbearable loss of personal love (24:15–18). He is not simply a divine mouthpiece; he is a wounded witness. His body becomes the site where divine pain is refracted, enacted, and delayed. The prophet does not explain trauma—he archives it. The scroll, in this light, becomes a vessel of deferred testimony.

Traumatized Characters

The exilic community within the narrative shares this condition. Their speech is rare, their agency minimal. When they do speak, their words are often cited by YHWH only to be rebuked (e.g., 12:22–23; 18:2). They exist as those who "have ears but do not hear"—not out of rebellion alone, but out of spiritual exhaustion. The trauma of displacement, temple loss, and historical rupture renders them mute, skeptical, or numb. They are not merely the recipients of judgment; they are the bearers of collective disorientation.

Traumatized Readers

Modern readers—especially those shaped by

135

war, displacement, inherited religious pain, or even ecclesial abuse—often approach Ezekiel with similar ambivalence. The harshness of judgment, the distance of God, and the deferred nature of hope can feel eerily familiar. For these readers, the scroll's unresolved grief does not need to be explained away—it needs to be recognized. The silence within the text becomes a mirror for their own deferred language of lament.

Toward Mutual Recognition

Yet within this shared fracture lies a possibility. If Ezekiel is a traumatized scribe, if his audience within the text is a traumatized people, and if we are, in part, traumatized readers, then the function of the text shifts. It is no longer a static proclamation of divine will. It becomes a dialogical archive—a place where trauma is not solved, but named; where grief is not denied, but held.

Healing, in such a model, comes not from immediate resolution but from reciprocal recognition. The prophet's obedience, the community's silence, and the reader's unsettled questions all participate in a sacred transmission. Each bears witness to the others. And in doing so, they open the possibility of a future response: one that consoles without dismissing, remembers without romanticizing, and honors suffering without allowing suffering to have the final word.

Conclusion

Ezekiel's body, broken and unread, becomes a sacred wound—a place where divine intention and human limitation collide. Rather than explain suffering, the scroll embodies it. Rather than resolve trauma, it records it.

To read Ezekiel is to sit with this embodied lament — not to interpret it away, but to join its silence, to trace its outlines, and perhaps, to be changed by its refusal to soothe. The prophet becomes not a hero of faith, but a bearer of fracture — through whom God's unresolved presence still speaks.

Chapter 8
Preaching Ezekiel in Ruins and Re-entry

Preaching from Ezekiel is not a task for those who seek to explain away complexity. It is a calling to dwell with divine disruption and give voice to unresolved hope. In a text where presence is mobile, audiences are fractured, and the prophet disappears into silence, the preacher does not close the scroll but reopens it.

To preach Ezekiel is to walk among ruins — not as a builder, but as a witness. The preacher is not Ezekiel, not YHWH, and not the remnant. She is the one who overhears. The task is not to restore confidence, but to restore attentiveness — to help communities hear what God once said when the world collapsed, and what God might still be saying when restoration remains out of reach.

From Interpreter to Participant

Traditional homiletics often casts the preacher as a mediator between biblical text and modern audience — interpreting, contextualizing, and applying. But with Ezekiel, this model falters. The prophet's silence, his unreceived oracles, his unmourned losses, and his ritualized grief resist mediation. They demand participation.

Preaching Ezekiel requires the preacher to become a reader-witness — one who re-enters the text's discomforts, not to explain them away but to be formed by them. It is a hermeneutics of proximity: not "what does this mean," but "what does this make to me?"

Ezekiel's scroll forms those who dare dwell with it — not with clarity, but with readiness.

Ministry in Delay

Ezekiel models a ministry that is suspended, deferred, and unacknowledged. The prophet delivers messages whose audience hardly responds, enacts signs no one comments on, and records words for a future that may not come. And yet, he remains faithful — not because of outcomes, but because of divine commissioning.

This is deeply relevant to contemporary ministry in contexts of spiritual fatigue, communal rupture, or institutional decline. Ezekiel reframes prophetic success away from measurable response toward faithful witness. He teaches that silence is not failure, but a form of fidelity.

Preaching in Exile: Five Practices

To preach from Ezekiel is to step into a space of rupture — where speech falters, bodies absorb meaning, and divine presence hides as much as it reveals. Ezekiel's scroll demands a different kind of homiletic posture: one that does not resolve but accompanies; one that neither silences trauma nor rushes healing. The following five practices offer a framework for preaching Ezekiel in the spirit of exilic faithfulness.

Resist Resolution: Let the Text Remain Tense

Ezekiel refuses to offer easy closure. Its metaphors remain unclarified, its judgments unresolved, and its visions deferred. Preachers must resist the impulse to domesticate these tensions. Do not soften divine violence, over-explain symbolism, or fill theological silences too quickly. Allow space for ambiguity and interruption. In doing so, the sermon becomes not a solution but a holding space for divine dissonance and human honesty.

Honor the Body: Let the Messenger Embody the Message

Ezekiel's prophetic acts are not merely verbal; they are deeply corporeal. His silence, posture, and movement carry the weight of divine intention. Likewise, preaching today is not only about what is said, but how the body speaks. Tone, gesture, stillness, and breath matter. The preacher's body becomes a secondary text, performing the tension, grief, or hope embedded in the scroll.

Name the Trauma: Speak What Others Avoid

Ezekiel names collapse without euphemism. He speaks of the temple's defilement, the people's desolation, and God's withdrawal with unnerving clarity. Contemporary preachers are invited to do the same. When congregations face spiritual apathy, ecclesial fragmentation, or cultural denial, sermons must speak with unflinching compassion. Truthful preaching does not retraumatize; it testifies.

Engage the Ecology of Displacement: Attend to Place as Theological Text

In Ezekiel, the land hears before the people do (Ezek 36). God addresses mountains, rivers, and soil as if they were animate partners in covenant. Preaching must likewise attend to the ecology of displacement — the sanctity of scarred spaces, the resonance of ruins, the meaning of place lost and reimagined. Restoration is not only spiritual but spatial. God's presence may move beyond the temple, but it never exits creation.

Invite Without Closure: Embrace the Unfinished Wait

Ezekiel ends not with a return but with a vision.

The new temple was drawn but never built. The city is renamed, but no one has yet entered. The sermon, likewise, should not declare that healing has arrived. Instead, it should witness to divine endurance and offer space for held breath. When God stops, we stop. When God marks time in silence, we wait with Him. The preacher becomes the one who holds the sheep close until the Shepherd returns.

Conclusion

Ezekiel is not just about what to preach. It is about what preaching is. The scroll insists that ministry be neither triumphant nor disembodied. It must be enacted, endured, and sometimes grieved.

The preacher is neither the glory nor the people, but the one who remembers — and bears witness to — what was seen. Like Ezekiel, preachers today carry scrolls full of fire, paradox, and sacred delay. We are not called to solve the text, but to hold it intact — even when no one seems to listen. This is preaching in exile. This is the Ministry of Ruins.

Chapter 9
From Hamon-Gog to YHWH Shammah
Ezekiel's Architecture of Preventing Return

The Book of Ezekiel is often read as a scroll of deferred communication, shaped by exile and rhetorical dislocation. Yet beyond its communicative architecture lies a more structural concern: how to prevent relapse into covenantal failure. From the grotesque burial site of Hamon-Gog (Ezek 39) to the utopian city of YHWH *Shammah* (Ezek 48), Ezekiel drafts a moral cartography wherein divine presence becomes sustainable only through strategic distance, ritual saturation, and visualized shame. This is not eschatological idealism— it is preventive theology.

The Fundamental Issue and Fundamental Solution: Divine Restoration, Human Recidivism

At the heart of Ezekiel's prophetic theology lies a paradox both sobering and hopeful: YHWH will restore His people, but they may relapse again. Ezekiel does not envision a naïve utopia or a permanently reformed people. Instead, the scroll builds toward a vision of restoration carefully structured to guard against recurring unfaithfulness—a vision not of perfect sanctity, but of preventive holiness. This is why partitions, measurements, and silence define the final temple. The restoration of divine presence (Ezekiel 43) is real, but it is also risky. God returns—but only after deep purification.

The core human problem, then, is recidivism— a stubborn pattern of betrayal masked by religious nostalgia or institutional complacency. This is not simply a matter of moral weakness; it is the failure to reckon with the depth of one's estrangement from God. In this sense, the fundamental issue is not just sin, but forgetfulness of how grievous the breach was — forgetfulness that leads to repetition.

Against this background, Ezekiel proposes a surprising solution: not stricter law, nor new rituals alone, but shame. "Then you will remember your evil ways... and loathe yourselves for your iniquities" (Ezekiel 36:31). The people must feel shame — but not as social disgrace or enemy-inflicted humiliation. They must experience ethical, internalized shame: the quiet ache that comes when one finally sees what God endured to stay.

This shame is not a tool of divine cruelty. It is a sign of relational awakening. The people had assumed God's anger was irrational, or that He was simply overpowered by Babylon's gods. Their trauma had distorted their theology. But when they come to understand that YHWH was not defeated, but restrained, not vengeful, but wounded — choosing to bear desecration to one day dwell with them again — then shame transforms from a weapon to a mirror.

This is the fundamental solution: not to prevent all future failure, but to create a restored relationship grounded in shared memory and mutual pain. The people's shame becomes the space in which they finally understand divine compassion — not as softness, but as costly restraint. In this way, God replaces the shame imposed by enemies with the sorrow that comes from insight. It is no longer about what Babylon did to them, but about what they did to YHWH, and what YHWH bore to be with them still.

Thus, the end of Ezekiel's vision is not romanticized reconciliation, but a solemn, sustainable communion. The people are not innocent — but they are no longer forgetful. Their shame is not condemnation—it is consecration. And in that holy regret, the cycle may not be broken, but it is remembered—and in remembering, redeemed.

The *Miqdash Me'at*: Holding Presence in Exilic Suspension

Between divine restoration and human relapse lies a long, suspended middle—exile not merely as punishment, but as spiritual incubation. In this liminal zone, the *Miqdash Me'at* (Ezekiel 11:16)—God's "little sanctuary among the exiles"—functions not as a replacement for the temple, but as a relational tether. It is sacred accommodation: a covenantal presence proportioned to human fragility, a gesture of divine endurance that allows the people to survive their shame without severing the bond.

This "little sanctuary" is not defined by space but by shared bearing. YHWH, having withdrawn from the polluted temple, does not abandon His people to fend for themselves; instead, He enters exile with them in diminished but intentional form. The *Miqdash Me'at* thus becomes a liminal theology of co-suffering: while the people reckon with their guilt and confusion, God restrains His full presence—not out of distance, but out of mercy. This compressed presence echoes the ethical logic of divine compassion: not indulgent proximity, but companionable endurance.

Critically, the *Miqdash Me'at* protects against both extremes: it prevents the people from clinging to the past as though nothing has changed, and it forestalls despair by signaling that restoration remains possible. It is a theological bridge—not between judgment and forgiveness in the abstract, but between collapse and reconstitution, guilt and intimacy. In the waiting, the people do not need a rebuilt temple; they need a renewed sense that God is with them, even in constrained form.

145

In the logic of Ezekiel, the people must become worthy to remember, and God must choose to be remembered in places of fragmentation. This mutual remembering is what transforms a little sanctuary into an eternal covenantal dwelling. The *Miqdash Me'at* thus prefigures a theology of divine proximity that does not demand rebuilt structures, but re-attuned hearts — hearts that have passed through fire, silence, and shame, and have come to desire not merely God's rescue, but God's nearness.

Hamon-Gog: Geography of Shame and Memory

Ezekiel 39 introduces a peculiar burial site: "the valley of those who pass by, east of the sea" (39:11). This valley — Hamon-Gog — is not merely a mass grave; it is a spatial device of theological pedagogy. Its location "on the road of passersby" suggests public visibility. The remains of divine judgment are not hidden but preserved as spectacle. The burial process itself — spanning seven months (39:12) and requiring communal participation — ritualizes memory. The task of marking bones (39:15) transforms every traveler into a participant in covenantal remembrance.

Theologically, Hamon-Gog functions as a "shame-device" — a site where the memory of past rebellion is neither erased nor venerated, but sedimented into the land itself. As with the Valley of Achor in Joshua and Hosea, this valley becomes a liminal space where judgment and hope converge. Yet, unlike Achor, Hamon-Gog offers no door of hope. It remains a sealed zone of memory. In this, it anticipates the function of Ezekiel's temple: not to reconcile shame, but to prevent its repetition.

YHWH *Shammah*: Presence without Possession

The city at the scroll's end bears a new name: "YHWH *Shammah*" ("The LORD is There," 48:35). But this is no return to Jerusalem. The name "Jerusalem" disappears from the vision altogether. The city is not the old throne restored, but a new gatepost installed. It exists as a sign rather than a destination. In this, YHWH *Shammah* is the narrative counterpoint to Hamon-Gog. One marks what must never return; the other signals what must never be presumed.

Both sites serve as theological terminals — boundary markers at the margins of human memory. The city is named for presence, yet no narrative records divine speech from within it. The presence is not performative; it is symbolic. Theologically, this implies a new covenantal stance: divine proximity without human access. Unlike Exodus or Kings, where divine presence correlates with dwelling, Ezekiel's conclusion reframes presence as spatial grammar. God is there — not for us to claim, but for us to approach only through rightly ordered shame.

Embodied Memory and Pedagogical Restraint: Learning and Preaching Ezekiel's Final Vision

To engage Ezekiel's closing vision is to confront a theology that prioritizes containment over climax, boundaries over belonging, and memory over immediacy. For teachers and preachers alike, this vision is both unsettling and instructive.

In the classroom, students often approach chapters 40–48 with impatience: the long cubits, the closed gates, the silent city. But when reframed as a ritual architecture of prevention, these elements reveal a different form of theological sophistication. The temple is not absent of meaning — it is saturated with ethical caution. A fruitful classroom exercise is to compare Ezekiel's temple with those of Exodus and Kings. What's missing is as instructive as what is present: no ark, no high priest's ephod, no communal festivals. The omissions are architectural sermons in

147

themselves.

From this angle, sacred space becomes a mode of instruction. One can ask: What does it mean for God to protect holiness not from human defilement but from human misremembrance? Ezekiel teaches that the divine is not only near but guarded—for our sake.

In the pulpit, these chapters demand a counterintuitive homiletic posture. The preacher is not called to soften the geometry, to spiritualize the silence, or to decode every gate. Instead, she is invited to preach presence without possession, to name the buried violence of history (Hamon-Gog), and to trace how God's faithfulness might look like distance rather than embrace.

One might imagine a sermon titled "The God Who Waits Outside the Gate"—drawing on the imagery of YHWH *Shammah*, a city not entered but named. Or a meditation on "The Valley We Pass By"—unpacking how divine memory remains lodged in a place we do not dwell but must acknowledge. Preaching from these texts is not about eschatological enthusiasm, but about ethical sobriety. Restoration here is not offered as a remedy but as a responsibility.

This is preaching toward containment: helping congregations carry the weight of divine presence with reverence, not entitlement. In Ezekiel's final vision, hope is not easy— it is exacting. And that is precisely its gift.

Conclusion

Ezekiel's final vision is not a dream of consummation, but a design of prevention. It forecloses the cycle of fall and return by embedding resistance into geography. Hamon-Gog ensures that death is remembered. The temple ensures that holiness is regulated. YHWH *Shammah* ensures that presence is never privatized. Together, they construct a theology of guarded proximity—a vision where memory disciplines hope, and architecture arrests relapse.

The Book of Ezekiel thus closes not with closure, but with containment. The scroll remains open, but its future is guarded. What Ezekiel offers is not a heaven come down, but a structure that remembers how quickly heaven is profaned. In a world of cyclic ruin, Ezekiel dreams not of paradise, but of a sanctuary strong enough to remember.

Conclusion to Part III
Memory as Resistance, Presence as Threat

Ezekiel ends not in triumph but in tension. His vision closes not with a feast, but with a city named *"YHWH is There"*—a city no one yet inhabits. The temple he describes is not warm with prayer, but cold with measurement. The land has been purged, but the shame remains. At the very threshold of restoration, Ezekiel builds barriers—not to resist hope, but to protect it from its own fragility.

Part III has traced Ezekiel's preventive imagination: where shame is spatialized, memory is ritualized, and divine presence is held at a distance. The prophet's body becomes the blueprint for a bruised theology. His audience is silenced—not to punish, but to deepen memory. His God returns—but stays behind gates. In Ezekiel, the cost of restoration is vigilance: the refusal to forget, to possess, or to presume.

These four chapters have argued that Ezekiel's most radical hope is not that Israel will return, but that Israel will not forget why it left. And that in remembering, Israel might remain near—not by touching the holy, but by honoring its flame.

Conclusion to the Volume
Ezekiel's Scroll, Still Unrolling
A Theology That Remembers Forward

The journey through Ezekiel's scroll, as undertaken in this volume, does not end with resolution, but with reverberation. To read Ezekiel is not to reach theological clarity or historical finality. It is to enter a prophetic world that performs rupture, enacts disorientation, and asks its readers to carry the unresolved.

Yet that is only part of the story. For Ezekiel is not merely a record of divine disruption—it is a theological construction site. The prophet does not simply name exile; he engineers structures to prevent its recurrence. His final vision is not a dream of restoration, but a system of restraint: an ethico-theological firewall. Through strategies of shame, limitation, distance, and spatial memory, Ezekiel reimagines how holiness might endure without being profaned again.

In Part I, we traced Ezekiel's displaced voice— emerging amid dislocation and collapse. He is no smooth-tongued messenger, but a silenced vessel through whom God's interruption becomes visible. His scroll does not persuade; it performs. It stores judgment as liturgy, memory as discipline.

In Part II, we examined selected passages as enacted theology. Symbol and silence, repetition and rupture, vision and architecture—all converged to express a divine pathos too volatile for exposition. Ezekiel trains his readers in delayed comprehension, forming them in the long echo of divine response.

In Part III, we turned to the prophet's preventive future. Chapters 6–9 shifted focus from exposition to architecture. Here, the scroll's most enduring contribution came into view: not a theology of return, but a cartography of resistance. Hamon-Gog, the temple's restrictive design, the silent city named YHWH *Shammah*—these are not endpoints, but theological mechanisms. They mark memory into landscape, embed shame into access, and withhold divine proximity not to alienate but to preserve.

Together, they gesture toward a prophetic landscape where presence and absence, trauma and hope, body and space remain in dynamic tension—a scroll still unfolding in the hands of its readers.

In Ezekiel, restoration is not the resolution of judgment—it is its continuation in disciplined form. Forgiveness demands remembrance. Proximity demands distance. Holiness, once defiled, must be approached only with reverent engineering.

What emerges is not a closed book, but an open tension—a scroll that refuses closure because it refuses amnesia. The scroll's audiences—exilic, remnant, future—are not merely invited to believe again, but to remember differently. Ezekiel's scroll is a liturgical object: it disciplines hope, names trauma, and redefines access to God's presence.

This volume has not sought to resolve Ezekiel's theological ruptures. Instead, it has lingered with them—critically, patiently, and constructively. The metaphors of violence, the architecture of distance, the vision of restoration-without-possession—all point to a theology that does not romanticize return but protects it from its own collapse.

We end, therefore, not with a summary, but with a charge. Ezekiel does not belong to the past. His scroll is still unrolling—for those who walk after rupture, for those who rebuild with caution, for those who worship with memory.

To carry Ezekiel's scroll is to commit to theological vigilance: to protect grace from amnesia, to name shame without paralysis, and to build spaces — liturgical, ethical, architectural — where the holy may dwell, and not be defiled.

To walk with this scroll is to bear its unresolved tensions: a presence that eludes permanence, a memory that guards against repetition, and a prophetic voice embodied amid histories of fracture. It is a scroll that resists closure, even as it invites our witness.

The scroll is still open. Let us walk with it — watchfully, faithfully, and without presumption.

Selected Bibliography

Allen, L. C. *Ezekiel 1–19*. Word Biblical Commentary 28. Dallas: Word Books, 1994.

Block, D. I. *The Book of Ezekiel, Chapters 1–24*. NICOT. Grand Rapids: Eerdmans, 1997.

Block, D. I. *The Book of Ezekiel, Chapters 25–48*. NICOT. Grand Rapids: Eerdmans, 1998.

Block, D. I. "In Search of Theological Meanings: Ezekiel Scholarship at the Turn of the Millennium." In *Ezekiel's Hierarchical World: Wrestling with a Tiered Reality*, edited by S. L. Cook & C. L. Patton, 227–39. SBLSymS 31. Atlanta, GA: Society of Biblical Literature, 2004.

Bodi, D. *The Book of Ezekiel and the Poem of Erra*. OBO 104; Freiburg/Schweiz: Universitätsverlag; Götting- en: Vandenhoeck & Ruprecht, 1991.

Brenner, A. *The Intercourse of Knowledge: On Gendering Desire and "Sexuality" in the Hebrew Bible*. Leiden: Brill, 1997.

Brownlee, W. H. "Ezekiel's Poetic Indictment of the Shepherds." *Harvard Theological Review* 51 (1958): 191–203.

Compton, R. A. "Spatial Possibilities for Reading Ezekiel 40–48: A Visionary and Textual Temple for a Priest in Exile." *Svensk Exegetisk Årsbok* 87 (2022): 141–64.

Cook, S. L. *Ezekiel 38–48: A New Translation with Introduction and Commentary*. AB 22B. New Haven: Yale University Press, 2022.

Darr, K. P. "The Wall Around Paradise: Ezekielian Ideas about the Future." *Vetus Testamentum* 37 (1987): 271–79.

Davis, E. F. *Swallowing the Scroll: Textuality and the Dynamics of Discernment in the Book of Ezekiel.* Louisville: Westminster John Knox, 1989.

Dijkstra, M. "The Valley of Dry Bones: Coping with the Reality of the Exile in the Book of Ezekiel." In *The Crisis of Israelite Religion: Transformation of Religious Tradition in Exilic and Post-Exilic Times*, edited by B. Becking & M. C. A. Korpel, 114–33. OTS 42. Leiden: Brill, 1999.

Dobbs-Allsopp, F. W. *Weep, O Daughter of Zion: A Study of the City-Lament Genre in the Hebrew Bible.* BibOr 44. Rome: Pontificio Istituto Biblico, 1993.

Duguid, I. M. *Ezekiel.* NIVAC. Grand Rapids: Zondervan, 1999.

Duguid, I. M. *Ezekiel.* Story of God Bible Commentary. Grand Rapids: Zondervan, 2023.

Frankel, D. "'I Gave Them Laws That Are Not Good' (Ezek 20:25): Divine Deception or Human Misunderstanding?" In *Theology of the Hebrew Bible, Volume 2: Texts, Readers, and Their Worlds*, edited by S. K. Sweeney (*et al.*), 199–214. RBS 107. Atlanta: SBL Press, 2024.

Friebel, K. G. *Jeremiah's and Ezekiel's Sign-Acts: Rhetorical Nonverbal Communication.* JSOTSup 283. Sheffield: Sheffield Academic Press, 1999.

Galambush, J. *Jerusalem in the Book of Ezekiel: The City as Yahweh's Wife.* SBL Dissertation Series 130. Atlanta: Scholars Press, 1992.

Ganzel, T. *Ezekiel's Visionary Temple in Babylonian Context.* Beihefte zur Zeitschrift für die alttestamentliche Wissenschaft 525. Berlin: De Gruyter, 2021.

Ganzel, T. "Ezekiel's Nonverbal Responses as Prophetic Message." *Zeitschrift für die Alttestamentliche Wissenschaft* 134 (2022): 179–92.

Greenberg, M. *Ezekiel 1–20*. AB 22. Garden City, NY: Doubleday, 1983.

Greenberg, M. *Ezekiel 21–37*. AB 22A. New York: Doubleday, 1997.

Hayes, E. R. – L.-S. Tiemeyer, eds. *'I Lifted My Eyes and Saw': Reading Dream and Vision Reports in the Hebrew Bible*. LHB/OTS 584. London and New York: Bloomsbury T&T Clark, 2014.

Hölscher, G. *Hesekiel: Kritisch bearbeitet*. Giessen: Töpelmann, 1924.

Joyce, P. M. *Divine Initiative and Human Response in Ezekiel*. Sheffield: JSOT Press, 1989.

Kim, S. J. "Ashamed Before the Presence of God: Shame in Ezekiel." In *Theology of the Hebrew Bible, Volume 1: Methodological Studies*, edited by M. A. Sweeney, 213–44. Atlanta: SBL Press, 2019.

Kim, S. J. "Was Ezekiel a Messenger? A Manager? Or a Moving Sanctuary? A Beckettian Reading of the Book of Ezekiel in the Inquiry of the Divine Presence." In *Partners with God: Theological and Critical Readings of the Bible in Honor of Marvin A. Sweeney*, edited by S. L. Birdsong & S. Frolov, 237–50. Claremont Studies in Hebrew Bible and Septuagint 2. Claremont, CA: Claremont Press, 2017.

Kim, S. J. "YHWH *Shammah*: The City as Gateway to the Presence of YHWH." *Journal for the Study of the Old Testament* 39.2 (2014): 213–30.

Lapsley, J. E. *Can These Bones Live? The Problem of the Moral Self in the Book of Ezekiel*. BZAW 301. Berlin: De Gruyter, 2000.

Lee, L. *Mapping Judah's Fate in Ezekiel's Oracles Against the Nations*. ANEM 15. Atlanta, GA: SBL Press and Centro de Estudios de Historia del Antiguo Oriente, 2016.

Levenson, J. D. *The Theology of the Program of Restoration of Ezekiel 40–48*. Missoula, MT: Scholars Press, 1976.

Liss, H. "'Describe the Temple to the House of Israel': Preliminary Remarks on the Temple Vision in the Book of Ezekiel and the Question of Fictionality in Priestly Literatures." In *Utopia and Dystopia in Prophetic Literature*, edited by E. Ben Zvi, 122–43. Publications of the Finnish Exegetical Society 92. Helsinki: The Finnish Exegetical Society; Göttingen: Vandenhoeck & Ruprecht, 2006.

Lust, J. "Exile and Diaspora: Gathering from Dispersion in Ezekiel." In *Lectures et relectures de la Bible: Festschrift P.-M. Bogaert*, edited by J.-M. Auwers & A. Wénin, 99–122. BETL 144. Leuven: Leuven University Press and Peeters, 1999.

Lyons, M. A. *From Law to Prophecy: Ezekiel's Use of the Holiness Code*. LHB/OTS 507. New York and London: T&T Clark International, 2009.

Marzouk, S. *Egypt as a Monster in the Book of Ezekiel*. Forschungen zum Alten Testament 2. Reihe 74. Tübingen: Mohr Siebeck, 2015.

Mayfield, T. "Literary Structure in Ezekiel 25: Address-ee, Formulas, and Genres." In *Partners with God: Theological and Critical Readings of the Bible in Honor of Marvin A. Sweeney*, edited by S. L. Birdsong & S. Frolov, 225–36. Claremont Studies in Hebrew Bible and Septuagint 2. Claremont, CA: Claremont Press, 2017.

Mayfield, T. D. & P. Barter, eds. *Ezekiel's Sign-Acts: Methods and Interpretation*. BZAW 562. Berlin: De Gruyter, 2025.

Mein, A. *Ezekiel and the Ethics of Exile*. Oxford Theological Monographs. Oxford: Oxford University Press, 2001.

Mein, A. & P. M. Joyce, eds. *After Ezekiel: Essays on the Reception of a Difficult Prophet*. LHB/OTS 535. New York and London: T&T Clark, 2011.

Mylonas, N. F. *Jerusalem as Contested Space in Ezekiel: A City's Transformation through the Prophetic Imagination*. LHBOTS 751. London: Bloomsbury T&T Clark, 2023.

Nevader, M. "YHWH and the Kings of Middle Earth: Royal Polemic in Ezekiel's Oracles against the Nations." In *Concerning the Nations: Essays on the Oracles Against the Nations in Isaiah, Jeremiah and Ezekiel*, edited by E. K. Holt (*et al.*), 161–78. LHB/OTS612. London andNewYork: Bloomsbury T&T Clark, 2015.

Nevader, M. "God of the Migrant: The Displacement of God in Ezekiel." In *Divine Displacement: Postcolonial Approaches to the Hebrew Bible*, edited by Samuel L. Boyd and Sarra Lev, 103–22. Sheffield: Sheffield Phoenix Press, 2022

Nihan, C. "Ezekiel and the Holiness Legislation – A Plea for Nonlinear Models." In *The Formation of the Pentateuch*, edited by J. C. Gertz (*et al.*), 1015–39. FAT 111. Tübingen: Mohr Siebeck, 2016.

Nihan, C. "Ezechiel 8 im Rahmen des Buches – Kompositions- und religionsgeschichtliche Aspekte." In *Das Buch Ezechiel: Komposition, Redaktion und Rezeption*, edited by J. C. Gertz (*et al.*), 89–124. BZAW 516. Berlin: De Gruyter, 2020.

Oded, B. "'Yet I Have Been to Them מעט למקדש in the Countries Where They Have Gone' (Ezekiel 11:16)." In *Sefer Moshe: The Moshe Weinfeld Jubilee Volume*, edited by C. Cohen (*et al.*), 103–14. Winona Lake, IN: Eisenbrauns, 2004.

Odell, M. S. *Ezekiel*. Smyth & Helwys Bible Commentary 16. Macon, GA: Smyth & Helwys, 2005.

Odell, M. S. "Ezekiel Saw What He Said He Saw: Genres, Forms, and the Vision of Ezekiel 1." In *The Changing Face of Form Criticism for the Twenty- First Century*, edited by M. A. Sweeney & E. Ben Zvi, 162–76. Grand Rapids, MI: Eerdmans, 2003.

Odell, M. S. & J. T. Strong, eds. *The Book of Ezekiel: Theological and Anthropological Perspectives*. SBLSymS 9. Atlanta, GA: Society of Biblical Literature, 2000.

Park, Y. B. *Restoration in the Book of Ezekiel: A Text- Linguistic Analysis of Ezekiel 33–39*. ACEBT Supplement Series 11. Bergambacht: 2VM, 2013.

Patton, C. L. "Priest, Prophet, and Exile: Ezekiel as a Literary Construct." In *Ezekiel's Hierarchical World: Wrestling with a Tiered Reality*, edited by S. L. Cook & C. L. Patton, 73–89. SBLSymS 31. Atlanta, GA: Society of Biblical Literature, 2004.

Poser, R. "Verwundete Prophetie: Das Ezechielbuch als Trauma-Literatur." In *»Gewaltig wie das Meer ist dein Zusammenbruch« (Klgl 2,13): theologische, psychologische und literarische Zugänge der Traumaforschung*, edited by D. Erbele-Küster (*et al.*), 119–31. Hermeneutische Untersuchungen zur Theologie 89. Tübingen: Mohr Siebeck, 2022.

Renz, T. *The Rhetorical Function of the Book of Ezekiel*. VTSup 76. Leiden: Brill, 1999.

Rom-Shiloni, D. "Ezekiel as the Voice of the Exiles and Constructor of Exilic Ideology." *Hebrew Union College Annual* 76 (2005): 1–45.

Rom-Shiloni, D. – C. L. Carvalho, eds. *Ezekiel in Its Babylonian Context*. Die Welt des Orients 45.1. Göttingen: Vandenhoeck & Ruprecht, 2015.

Schwartz, B. J. "Ezekiel's Dim View of Israel's Restoration." In *The Book of Ezekiel: Theological and Anthropological Perspectives*, edited by M. S. Odell & J. T. Strong, 43–67. SBLSymS 9. Atlanta, GA: Society of Biblical Literature, 2000.

Stevenson, K. R. *The Vision of Transformation: The Territorial Rhetoric of Ezekiel 40–48*. SBLDS 154. Atlanta, GA: Scholars Press, 1996.

Stovell, B. M. "Yahweh as Shepherd-King in Ezekiel 34: A Linguistic-Literary Analysis of Metaphors of Shepherding." In *Modeling Biblical Language*, edited by S. E. Porter (*et al.*), 200–230. Linguistic Biblical Studies 13. Leiden: Brill, 2016.

Stravrakopoulou, F. "Exploring the Gardens of Uzza: Death, Burial and Ideologies of Kingship." *Biblica* 87 (2006): 1–21.

Stavrakopoulou, F. "Gog's Grave: Ezekiel 39 and Ancient Israelite Funerary Practices." *Biblical Interpretation* 15.1 (2007): 44–64.

Strine, C. A. "Ritualized Bodies in the Valley of Dry Bones (Ezekiel 37.1–14)." In *The Body in Biblical, Christian and Jewish Texts*, edited by J. E. Taylor, 41–57. LSTS 85. London and New York: Bloomsbury T&T Clark, 2014.

Strine, C. A. "The Role of Repentance in the Book of Ezekiel: A Second Chance for the Second Generation." *Journal of Theological Studies* NS 63 (2012): 467–491.

Strine, C. A. "Imitation, Subversion, and Transformation of the Mesopotamian Mīs Pî Ritual in the Book of Ezekiel's Depiction of Holy Space." In *Holy Places in Biblical and Extrabiblical Traditions*, edited by J. Flebbe, 65–78. BBB 179. Göttingen: V&R unipress / Bonn University Press, 2016.

Strine, C. A. (*et al.*), eds. *Dialectics of Displacement: Scriptural Approaches to Migrant Experience.* Sheffield: Sheffield Phoenix Press, 2017.

Strong, J. T. "Egypt's Shameful Death and the House of Israel's Exodus from Sheol (Ezekiel 32.17–32 and 37.1–14)." *Journal for the Study of the Old Testament* 34.4 (2010): 475–504.

Sweeney, M. A. "The Destruction of Jerusalem as Purification in Ezekiel 8–11." In *Form and Intertextuality in Prophetic and Apocalyptic Literature*, 144–155. FAT 45. Tübingen: Mohr Siebeck, 2005.

Sweeney, M. A. "Eschatology in the Book of Ezekiel." In *Making a Difference: Essays on the Bible and Judaism in Honor of Tamara Cohn Eskenazi*, edited by D. J. A. Clines (*et al.*), 277–91. Hebrew Bible Monographs 49. Sheffield: Sheffield Phoenix Press, 2012.

Sweeney, M. A. *Reading Ezekiel: A Literary and Theological Commentary.* Macon, GA: Smyth & Helwys, 2013.

Sweeney, S. K. "Communications of the Book of Ezekiel: From the Iron Wall to the Voice in the Air." In *The Oxford Handbook of Ezekiel*, edited by C. L. Carvalho, 312–29. Oxford: Oxford University Press, 2023.

Sweeney, S. K. "Rattling Noises in the Dry Bone Plain: Ezekiel 37 and the Theology of Resurrection." In *Theology of the Hebrew Bible, Volume 2: Texts, Readers, and Their Worlds*, edited by S. K. Sweeney (*et al.*), 183–98. RBS 107. Atlanta: SBL Press, 2024.

Tooman, W. A. – M. A. Lyons, eds. *Transforming Visions: Transformations of Text, Tradition, and Theology in Ezekiel*. Princeton Theological Monograph Series 127. Eugene, OR: Pickwick Publications, 2010.

Tooman, W. A. – P. Barter, eds. *Ezekiel: Current Debates and Future Directions*. FAT 112. Tübingen: Mohr Siebeck, 2017.

Tuell, S. S. "The Priesthood of the 'Foreigner': Evidence of Competing Polities in Ezekiel 44:1–14 and Isaiah 56:1–8." In *Constituting the Community: Studies on the Polity of Ancient Israel in Honor of S. Dean McBride, Jr.*, edited by J. T. Strong & S. S. Tuell, 183–204. Winona Lake, IN: Eisenbrauns, 2008.

Zimmerli, W. *Ezechiel*. Biblischer Kommentar Altes Testament XIII/1–2. Neukirchen-Vluyn: Neukirchener Verlag, 1969–1979.

www.ingramcontent.com/pod-product-compliance
Lightning Source LLC
La Vergne TN
LVHW051057080426
835508LV00019B/1936